PARENTING IN THE

Smart Zone

Submit all requests for reprinting to:
Greenleaf Book Group LLC
4425 Mopac South, Suite 600
Longhorn Bldg., 3rd Floor
Austin, TX 78735
(512) 891-6100

Published in the United States by
Susan Fletcher, Ph.D.
Plano, TX

www.HearSusan.com
www.FletcherPhD.com

Layout by Stephanie Milanoski
Illustrations by Allison Pickett and Jasmine Ojeda
Cover design by Mark Dame
First Edition

To the many families who have trusted me with their private lives . . . in the painful times as well as during the successes. I am truly grateful.

Acknowledgments

My family has been supportive of the hours it has taken me to complete this book. My husband Mark has believed in my passion to get this on paper. Thank you for picking up the slack, going to our children's practices without me, cooking dinner, and waking me up when I have fallen asleep while laying down with the kids. You made this possible.

To my kids Alex, Chase and Sam. You have changed my world forever and your wellbeing is my top priority. You make me proud.

To my parents and grandparents, I appreciate your encouragement, your support, and belief in me. You created a monster that feels the need to produce and go for more. As the poster in my room growing up said, "Anything worth doing is worth doing right." I was listening.

To our friends and Mark's family, thanks for excusing me for being so focused and committed to my practice, this book and to speaking. Our children are lucky to have you all in our lives.

I also am so appreciative of my professional and personal relationship with Trudy Bourgeois. Thanks for being my accountability partner and my friend. You get it and I cherish our time and our projects.

Most of all, I owe so much gratitude to my assistant Sharon Beck. I appreciate your no nonsense approach to work and for sharing the belief that family always comes first. I want everyone to know I could not have done this without you. Your attention to this project and all the projects in the last two years is invaluable.

Finally, I am extremely appreciative of the opportunity I had to work with Dr. Phil McGraw.

Table of Contents

✳ Introduction

I Was the Best Parent
until I Had Kids

In the summer of 1995, I had a lot to look forward to: I had finally completed all of the coursework needed to earn my Ph.D. in psychology; I had finished my one-year internship in Fort Worth, splitting my time between the Child Study Center and the Fort Worth School District; I was feeling competent about my skills as a psychologist, and I was getting a lot of support and encouragement from supervisors, university faculty, colleagues, family, and friends. I knew that I could make it in the field of psychology.

My husband and I also felt we were reaching a milestone. We had decided to wait to have children until after I graduated. I had seen so many of my friends in graduate school battle the commitments of family and academics that I knew I would have a hard time trying to be the ultimate parent when so much was required of me as a Ph.D. candidate. When the time was right, I wanted to be the best parent I could be.

That last year of schooling was a feat in and of itself. I wasn't planning to do my internship that year. Instead, I had chosen to wait a year so I could finish my dissertation and continue to build up a healthy patient base in private practice in Plano, Texas. I thought it would be hard to work in a low-paying internship position, while at the same time devoting my energy to building a private practice. Both would require significant energy and attention, while boasting a high-level learning curve.

After the deadlines had passed for internships, a new position was created for an intern willing to split his or her time between two settings. This internship was a unique opportunity that offered the candidate learning opportunities and exposure working with pediatricians, experienced psychologists, occupational therapists, physical therapists, speech therapists, and psychiatrists. I applied, was interviewed over Memorial Day weekend, and began my internship in August 1994.

Fort Worth was sometimes an hour-and-a-half commute from our home in Plano. If traffic was particularly fluid, I could get there successfully in less than an hour. As the first few months of the internship year progressed, I would put in a full day in Fort Worth and then hightail it back to Plano at least two days a week to see a few patients at the private practice. Saturdays were also working days. By offering Saturday appointments, I could easily see six or seven people in one day. By

Sunday, I was tired, but I was willing to do whatever I needed to in order to have a good internship experience and build up my client base. I wanted to continue to improve my skills, learn from the best, and slowly build a private practice so I would have a job when I graduated in August 1995. A job meant a steady referral base that could one day lead to a successful, independent private practice. I had to cover a lot of ground during that year to encourage people to refer their friends, family, and coworkers to me. People only see a psychologist when they need to, and I wanted to be the name people thought of when they entertained the idea of going to therapy. I had so many things to be proud of and look forward to. My internships were going well, graduation was approaching, and my husband and I had our plan: we would start a family as soon as I graduated.

Then there was that night in October 1994. My husband's cousin Ben was living with us temporarily after getting a master's in English from the University of Alabama. While Ben stayed with us, we had many conversations about how to have a fulfilling life while keeping the simple things in the forefront.

After sharing a bottle of wine and some deep conversation with Ben, my husband and I retreated to our bedroom. All it took was the question, "Wouldn't it be neat to tell our families at Christmas that we are pregnant?

After all those years of trying so hard not to get pregnant while I was in graduate school, you would think it wouldn't happen the first time we truly tried. Two weeks before Christmas, though, I found out I was pregnant and that I was due on August 20, one week after my August 13 graduation date.

Alexander Henderson Fletcher, the first of our three boys, was born on his due date of August 20, 1995. We had just barely kept to our plan and waited to have children until after I graduated with my Ph.D.

I graduated the week before Alexander was born. Family and friends cheered me on as I received my Ph.D. I wore the ceremonial Ph.D. regalia, complete with a graduation gown that draped awkwardly over my bulky middle. On that day in 1995, I moved my tassel and gave hugs to my proud professors. I never felt more competent in my life. Then seven days later, I gave birth to my first child. The epidural didn't work, and I failed to convince the anesthesiologist that my labor hurt like hell. I began to feel less competent. As the days progressed my husband and I continued to find ourselves challenged by parenthood. We thought we would make the best parents until we had children. Suddenly, our expectations were put to the test.

This is not a book about how to parent children with clinical disorders or about how to raise children. While strategies for raising children are found throughout, the focus is on parents and their expectations, and how parents can stay in their most productive mode—their SMART Zone. I hope this book guides you to becoming the best parent you can be—especially now that you have kids.

Working in Your SMART Zone

Hopefully, all of us are trying to live life the best way we know how. Whether it is in our role as parents, in our jobs, in our marriages, or with the other responsibilities in life, we each have the opportunity to function at our best level. Yet, after more than fourteen years of practicing psychology, I have seen a powerful trend. Patients often come into my office saying, "I don't feel like myself." They tell tales of being preoccupied, overlooking things at work, and having trouble thinking ahead. They make decisions or act impulsively, without really considering if their actions are in their best interests. There are many examples of how their professional and personal lives are affected. For some people, there are clinical issues to address. For others, there are better habits that could be adopted. Nevertheless, when it comes to raising children, we can all benefit from learning ways to parent more successfully.

I call this parenting in the SMART Zone. The SMART Zone is the mental state for optimal performance using intellect, emotions, and behaviors. Therefore, parenting in the SMART Zone is a simple concept: you know your expectations, philosophies, and goals as a parent so that you function to the best of your ability—in your SMART Zone. The hard part is adjusting your expectations. This book will provide you with a set of scenarios, questions, and examples in order to help you function in your own, unique and productive SMART Zone.

I believe that we can each focus, think things through, and manage ourselves effectively in our day-to-day lives, despite the influence worry, stress, and dissatisfaction can have on our relationships. For parents, this can mean being aware of your expectations and how they can potentially interfere with your ability to function in your SMART Zone. It also means recognizing how your philosophy, your actions, your discipline strategies, and the type of parent you want to be might need to be adjusted to put you in your SMART Zone.

When I really looked at those people who operated outside of the SMART Zone, I began to see it as an obstacle to productivity. In our personal lives, operating outside of the SMART Zone can interfere with our parenting and decrease satisfaction in other relationships. In our professional lives, it can decrease our productivity and, ultimately, our profits. It was as though bright people were not working to their full potential, including parents who were parenting without really thinking their actions through. Outside of their SMART Zone, they couldn't figure out why there were problems, when they thought they were doing the best they could.

People working outside of their SMART Zone are essentially working below their IQ. Over time, I have concluded—and research supports—that worry and stress drain intelligence and hold back performance, leading to ineffectiveness. Working to eliminate worry, stress, depression, and frustration improves performance and increases satisfaction in relationships. Using this idea in my clinical practice, I have seen inspiring changes in people who previously believed something was "wrong" with them. I can help people parent more successfully by readjusting their expectations of themselves as parents, which, in turn, keeps them in their SMART Zone.

Chapter 1

SMART Parenting:
It Can't Be That Hard

From afar, it is easy to think we can do a better job than someone else. You might have had this experience watching *Jeopardy*, driving in traffic, or waiting on slow service at a bad restaurant. Think about poor Steve Bartman, the Cubs fan who reached out and caught the ball intended for outfielder Moises Alou in the fall of 2003. We all want to believe that we wouldn't have made the same mistake. But what about when it comes to SMART parenting? Do we really think we can do a better job than our parents, our neighbors, or even our friends?

Most couples probably talk about having children before they get married. For those couples who agree that they want to have children, typically, there is a discussion about discipline, schooling, and even what names to consider. But when you don't know what you don't know, you also don't know what kind of conversations to have. Most people's only parenting course was being raised by their own parents. This dynamic influences people's expectations of themselves as parents in a multitude of ways.

Most of the time, being raised by your own parents isn't enough to help you flesh out a realistic expectation of parenting. That is why it is important to define your own expectations in order to develop a SMART parenting philosophy.

Whether a couple is planning to get married, is already married but has not yet had children, are pregnant and expecting their first child, or are already raising four kids, having a SMART parenting philosophy is like having a mission statement. When corporations merge they have to develop their unique business plan; why should it be any different for couples merging their expectations as parents?

What Is a SMART Parenting Philosophy?

It isn't an agreement on how to punish. It isn't about the choice of private versus public school. It is the voice that guides all decisions and interactions—especially the everyday interactions—and it is the most important influence on a parent's expectations.

Without a SMART parenting philosophy, parents tend to:
- Treat each event as distinct, isolated, and independent from other related events
- Focus on the major decisions as the most important decisions, often to the exclusion of other smaller, everyday decisions
- Micromanage their children with poor results
- See themselves as the greatest influence in their children's lives
- See the influence of others as insignificant
- Overcommit children to too many activities
- Let children decide for themselves what is best for them
- Focus on the ends that justify the means
- Allow children to have greater success pitting one parent against another
- Run the risk of trying to be friends with their children at the expense of being able to discipline their child effectively

With a SMART parenting philosophy, parents can:
- Treat each event as an opportunity
- Realize that minor decisions and interactions are just as important as big ones
- Foster independence with better long-term results
- Create environments conducive to change that influence their children to make good decisions
- Welcome a team approach and seek out others who will be positive influences on their children
- Choose activities as part of a greater whole
- Allow a child's input in order to help that child build a set of independent skills
- Focus on the means to an end
- Have a greater strategic alliance with their spouse or significant other
- Enjoy friendliness with their children, while clearly retaining the role as a parent

When we take on a new position at work, we get a job description listing our responsibilities. We adjust our leadership style to reflect the image and philosophy of the company we represent. Becoming a parent is much like beginning a new job. The responsibilities and philosophies should be discussed and somewhat defined before birth. However, it is also important to realize that most philosophies are not easily agreed upon, especially between the parent and the child. A parent-child relationship, just like business relationships, can be both volatile and, at times, uncooperative.

Thinking Less about Technique

There is a plethora of information available about the techniques used to raise children, including the methods used to raise a critical thinker, the fine art of "time out," and the expert skill of redirecting a child's behavior. While these tactics are important, their success can be short lived if the philosophical model is not well developed and intact. When parents come to my office for therapy, or ask questions after they hear me speak, they typically start with queries such as, "How many minutes should a three-year-old stay in time out?" Another typical question is, "What do I do if my wife interrupts me while I am trying to punish the kids?"

No matter what the question, I always respond by asking, "What are you trying to accomplish?" "I'm trying to get my five-year-old to stop hitting his sister" is a good answer; but the better answer reflects more than just the behavior a parent wants to change; it encompasses the parenting philosophy, the values, and life skills a parent wants to instill. If you consider a brother hitting his sister as an opportunity to teach respect for another person and the importance of managing one's emotions, a parent can cover a wider range of successful results.

When it is about respect rather than just "not hitting," parenting is far more successful. It is parenting in the SMART Zone.

Steps to Developing a SMART Parenting Philosophy

You are raising the parents of your grandchildren.

That statement gets a lot of people thinking. It is an interesting concept. Remember, if you are like most of us, your only parenting course was being raised by your own parents; perhaps the thought that you are now teaching your own children about parenting compounds the importance of the SMART parenting philosophy tenfold.

For families with parents raising their children together, SMART parenting philosophies are best developed through cooperation and collaboration. Collaboration is still possible for parents who are separated or divorced, but as you can imagine, or have experienced, it can be more difficult to follow similar philosophies. Finally, single parents, especially those who are overextended by raising a family alone, have the added difficulty of shouldering most of the responsibility. In 2002, according to the United States Census Bureau, 69 percent of children lived with two parents; 23 percent lived with only their mother; 5 percent lived with only their father; and another 4 percent lived in households with neither parent present. Of course, there are challenges no matter what the family situation; the various transitions in a family and the range of parental influences simply reinforce the importance of having a solid parenting philosophy to begin with.

Kathy is a single parent raising two boys, ages eight and six. She and their father split as soon as their second child was born. It is difficult for Kathy and her ex-husband to communicate, especially since he quickly remarried a woman who does not want the complication of being a stepmother. At best, the new stepmother tolerates the weekend visits with her stepchildren. Therefore, Kathy finds herself having to develop her SMART parenting philosophy without the collaboration of her children's father.

While she would never have wished to be a divorced mother of two, Kathy believes she has no choice but to view a single-parent household as an opportunity. She sees her boys as having the chance to be members of a team; she attempts to instill a sense of ownership for the chores they are responsible for and the contributions they make to help the family run smoothly. While she doesn't hold them accountable for tasks that are inappropriate for their age, she does create situations where they are more likely to feel a sense of pride for their contributions. For her eight-year-old, that means taking the trash out, carrying groceries in from the car, and helping to cook favorite meals. For her six-year-old, it means feeling a sense of accomplishment by feeding the dog, setting the table, and cutting coupons out of the newspaper. Instead of simply telling her children, "I am so proud of you," she fosters an internal sense of pride by adding, "Aren't you proud of yourself?" As a single mother, Kathy wants her sons to believe in themselves and not rely on external factors, including other people, to make them feel good.

Sometimes a parent might question their ability to parent. Other people may make it look effortless and it is easy to get worn down. As Eleanor Roosevelt remarked, "Nobody makes you feel inferior unless you give them permission." If a parent starts thinking they are ineffective, then they are sure to have trouble staying in their SMART Zone.

> *To stay in their SMART Zone, I encourage parents to ask themselves:*
> • What are the core values I want to instill?
> • What kinds of experiences will reinforce those values?
> • Are the choices I am making for my child consistent with
>   those values?
> • What influences are available to reinforce those values?
> • Do I reinforce those values as a role model?
> • Once my children become adults, how will they finish the
>   statement, "My parents instilled in me . . .?"

Asking these questions can help you begin to define your parenting philosophy. Knowing your expectations and having a parental mission statement will help you stay productive as a parent in your SMART Zone.

What Influences Our Expectations and the Development of Our SMART Parenting Philosophy?

Make no mistake about it. You don't just choose the concepts in your SMART parenting philosophy from a menu. Similarly, you don't always know why you have certain expectations when it comes to parenting. A number of factors influence people's SMART parenting philosophies and their expectations of parenting. Some have a positive influence on parenting, and others have a negative influence. Examples include:

1. A History of Abuse

Every ten seconds a child is abused in the United States. Abuse can be emotional, physical, or sexual, or it can come in the form of neglect. People who have suffered childhood abuse are often influenced by their past as they develop their SMART parenting philosophy. Their expectations of parenting may be shaped by fear of repeating a pattern, a preoccupation with control, or a tendency to feel emotionally overwhelmed by parenting. Their expectations of parenting can also be influenced by an inability to regulate the anger and frustration often precipitated by severe or even routine misbehavior in their own children.

2. Your Family of Origin

As I have already discussed, the family you were raised in, as well as the way you were raised, will influence your expectations of parenting. For example, if you are female and you were raised with sisters but no brothers, your expectations are going to be influenced. Expectations may also be skewed if you were raised in a family where you were the only child or you are a child of a divorce. According to the research of Judith Wallerstein, Ph.D., adult children of divorce tend to have a harder time dealing with even moderate conflict, are often more fearful of failure, are frequently more insecure about relationships, and are more likely to experience a divorce themselves.

3. Your Culture

Different religious backgrounds, ethnic influences, cultural norms, and regions of the United States heavily influence our expectations. For instance, families from the Middle East prefer and plan to integrate family members in influential parenting roles so grandparents may have just as much power over parenting as parents.

4. Your Training and Job Skills

When at least one parent is in a high-level, managerial job, they tend to try and run their household the way they run their business. It is not unusual to have a senior executive, male or female, say to me, "How come I do so well motivating my people to do the right thing at work, but I can't get my kids to do the smallest things at home?"

5. Your Self-Esteem

The best definition I have come across for self-esteem is this: self-esteem is the reputation we have with ourselves. It doesn't matter what other people think of us. If we think poorly of ourselves, our actions and expectations will probably reflect those thoughts.

6. Your Non-Negotiable Necessities

Non-negotiable necessities are your behaviors or preferences that reflect your core values that are difficult to bend or adjust that should be honored and respected. Going against them causes turmoil. As a parent you have non-negotiable necessities. While they may seem simple they are powerful and hard to bend. For example, a lot of people have a thing about having dirty dishes in the sink and needing them to be clean before going to bed. Even though there are reasons why it would be okay to leave a few dirty dishes in the sink and go on to sleep, some people just can't do it. It goes against their grain. It causes such uneasiness that it is easier (almost a release) to get them done and then go to bed. I feel that way about wet towels on the floor. My husband feels that way about clothes stacked on the bathroom counter. A friend of mine feels that way about sitting in a booth at a restaurant rather than at a table in the middle of the room. We all have non-negotiable necessities. Knowing what they are and assessing whether they have a positive influence or a negative influence on our parenting is important.

Merging SMART Parenting Philosophies

How do companies do it? They establish their business goals and then negotiate a means to an end. So often, parents bring children with behavior problems to therapy and they agree on the goal: to extinguish the inappropriate behavior. Yet the father may advocate spanking, while the mom wants to try and reason with their son, hoping his behavior will turn around for the better. If they can't agree on and develop their own unique SMART parenting philosophy, they can actually work against each other.

For example, Sherri believes that her son Jason's behavior is a symptom of "something." She tends to be more permissive and has a higher threshold for what can be considered disruptive behavior. When Jason refuses to pick up his toys, Sherri might ask him a few times to pick them up. If he doesn't oblige, Sherri might pick them up herself, believing that it is best to keep the peace at home.

On the other hand, Sherri's husband, Rick, has less tolerance for Jason's behavior. He thinks Jason can be downright disrespectful. Rick doesn't agree with Sherri's method of cutting him so much slack. He thinks that Sherri's method is the reason that Jason continues to misbehave. To compensate for her permissiveness, Rick tends to immediately opt for spanking. They are working against each other because they are not in sync with their SMART parenting philosophies.

If Sherri and Rick examine their SMART parenting philosophies, they might even find that their opposing actions, in conjunction with each other, are actually contributing to the escalation of Jason's misbehavior. The message Jason may be getting is, "I can get away with it with my mom, but I can't with my dad. In fact, my dad doesn't cut me any slack." Are they teaching Jason how to become a manipulator? I'm sure that teaching their son the fine art of manipulation is not part of their SMART parenting philosophy. Instead, Sherri and Rick need a collaborative philosophy, so that they are working together to raise their son and not contradicting one another.

The Responsibility of a SMART Parent

It can be challenging to look at our expectations of parenting and our expectations of ourselves. As I have seen with the many families I have worked with over the past fifteen years, challenging our own expectations and being flexible enough to make smart adjustments leads to a better experience as a parent and more successful parenting.

To enhance your experience, consider the following suggestions:
- View parenting as an experience rather than a task.
- Recognize the importance of your interactions, no matter how unimportant they may seem.
- Resist the tendency to take care of your children when it is always at your expense.
- Entertain the idea that your spouse or significant other may see faults you are unable (or unwilling) to see for yourself.
- Allow yourself to be somewhat influenced by the other parent's suggestions.
- Be willing to challenge your own expectations.
- Consider that you are raising the parents of your future grandchildren.
- Adjust your expectations for each of your children based on their individual abilities.
- See each interaction as an opportunity for change.
- Let your children fail; don't rob them of the chance to gain their own wisdom.

Following these simple suggestions can help keep your SMART Zone parenting in sync with your personal expectations and philosophies.

Chapter One
SMART Moves:

- Having a SMART parenting philosophy is like having a mission statement: develop your own unique parenting plan.

- Collaborate on the SMART parenting philosophy with your spouse. If you are a single parent, view the situation as an opportunity, and stick by your own solid philosophy.

- Recognize the factors that might shape your parenting philosophy.

- Be a role model and reinforce values for your children.

- View parenting as an experience rather than a task.

# Chapter 2

*Wanting to Give Your Kids
Everything You Didn't Have*

In an effort to give our kids what we didn't have, we sometimes forget to give them what we did have. We all think we can do it better than our parents did. But this is our kids' only experience growing up with parents who try to guide them successfully to adulthood.

Spoiling Your Kids

Many pediatricians say that it is impossible to spoil an infant. You simply can't give them too much attention. However, we all would agree that you can give them too little attention. But what about with a child or adolescent? Would you be able to recognize if you were spoiling them?

Bill grew up in Mississippi and was always around family. He had three brothers and each of them had their own share of difficulties. His oldest brother John smoked pot as a freshman in high school, but his parents didn't find out until John flunked out of his first year in college. By then, John's drug problem was pretty pervasive and well developed.

The next older brother, Jim, was smart but never really applied himself. Jim would rather play basketball than study, so his grades were always poor. His report card reflected the work he hadn't completed rather than an inability to do the work. Jim was always looking for something else to interest him because he couldn't care less about school. Jim was introduced to gambling before he left high school, and by the time he was twenty-two, he was deep in debt from betting on Sunday football games, the horses, and playing poker in back rooms of Mississippi bars. Bill's parents had to cover Jim's debts, and, Bill suspects, pay for Jim's apartment and car just so Jim wouldn't have to move back home.

Finally, Bill's brother Bobby was a mere three years older than Bill. He was born with good looks and developed a high sex drive. He lost his virginity at age fourteen and got two girls pregnant before he graduated high school. Both girls considered abortions, but the girls' families, having been raised in Mississippi and believing that abortion was not an option, agreed to help raise the two children. Bobby seemed oblivious to the responsibility of raising his children and was finally sued for child support after he turned eighteen. Bobby's parents weren't always sure if he paid it, and they mourned over having two grandchildren who would never be a part of their lives.

Genogram of Bill's Family

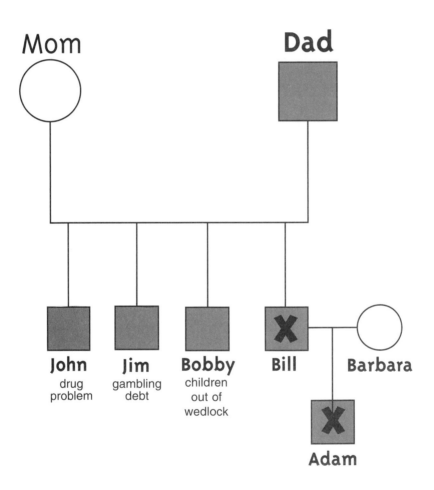

Bill was the youngest child. His upbringing was heavily influenced by the experience his parents had raising his three older brothers. Bill's parents didn't cut him any slack. They were determined to stop Bill from making the same mistakes his older brothers had made. They believed mandatory church attendance and limited social time would make him immune to the dangers of adolescence and young adulthood. Bill was seen as a good kid because he didn't cause problems, but he was given little freedom to create any. He did his own laundry, made his own meals, and had a job working in a gas station by the time he was twelve. He had to earn his own money in order to buy his first car. Bill always thought it was unfair that he wasn't allowed to make his own mistakes.

Bill married Barbara, whom he met in college. They graduated with master's degrees, saved money to buy their own home, and gave birth to a son named Adam. Adam was full of personality, and Bill felt as if he wanted his son to have some of the freedom he'd been denied. Because of infertility problems, Bill and his wife were lucky to have had any children at all. Perhaps this explains why Bill believed that putting all his energy into his son's upbringing would protect Adam from the evils of life, while at the same time giving him the freedom Bill thought Adam deserved.

Barbara and Bill argued all the time about what was in Adam's best interest. Bill had a great job that allowed Barbara to be a stay-at-home mom. That was Bill's preference and Barbara's desire, too; but they disagreed about how much Barbara should do for Adam once he was old enough to take on responsibility.

Barbara and Bill had different parenting philosophies. Bill believed that Adam would benefit from having things done for him so he could focus on his school work and social life. Bill's favorite phrase was, "He's only going to be a kid once, so let him be a kid." Barbara could see how Bill's perception of his own upbringing influenced his decisions about how they should raise Adam, but she believed Bill spoiled Adam and didn't give him the opportunity to learn from experience. In an effort to give his son what he hadn't had, Bill failed to give Adam what he had— the opportunity to develop those important life skills.

As an adult, Bill was financially responsible. He could be counted on. Barbara feared that Adam would have too much done for him and would not develop the ability to manage his life on his own.

Robbing Your Children of Their Own Wisdom

Parents shouldn't be afraid of seeing their children fail. Only by letting kids make mistakes under supervision do they allow their children to gain their own wisdom. As parents, it is difficult to watch our children suffer the consequences of those mistakes, as we fear that the repercussions will be too traumatic or life-changing for them.

It's possible that, after the experiences they had with their other three boys, Bill's parents went overboard by being so restrictive with him. They probably wouldn't have forgiven themselves if they believed that they'd neglected to raise Bill with very strict rules and guidelines in an effort to get him through his teenage years.

On the other hand, there is a case to be made for Bill swinging the pendulum too far the other way. Bill didn't want Adam doing his own laundry, having a job, or being given what he perceived as "adult" tasks until it was completely necessary. Barbara resented doing Adam's laundry and often felt like she was a slave put on this earth to make her son completely comfortable. Bill wouldn't budge and Adam went on to live a cushiony life.

After years of arguments between Barbara and Bill about how to raise Adam, the marital conflict took a toll. Barbara and Bill separated. That is when they came to marital therapy.

It was difficult to get Bill to talk about his marriage. He resented Barbara for not respecting the parenting choices he made, which he believed to be in Adam's best interest. While Bill and Barbara lived apart, Adam was somewhat unsupervised and he tended to play his parents against each other. Bill was humbled by Adam's missteps. He believed that Adam wouldn't make mistakes, because he knew better. As time went on, though, it became apparent that Adam didn't know better, as he hadn't been allowed to practice his own decision-making skills. He'd been sheltered from the opportunity to have better judgment.

It all came to a head when Adam got caught drinking in the Kroger parking lot in his Texas hometown. In Texas, if you get caught drinking and you are under twenty-one, you are charged with MIP—Minor in Possession. Adam was staying with his father that weekend and didn't have a curfew. Bill liked Adam's friends and believed that it was safe to allow Adam the freedom to be out as late as he wanted. When Bill got the call from the police officer to pick up his son in the middle of the night, he was sure that they were wrong. He couldn't believe that Adam would use such poor judgment.

Adam ended up getting sick all over himself, but even then he denied drinking alcohol and insisted that he must have a touch of the flu. The other boys, while guilty, were at least willing to admit that they had been drinking—although they all believed that the officer had gone overboard by giving them a citation.

The next day Bill had a talk with Adam and told him he was disappointed in his judgment the night before. Adam finally told him it had been the first time he ever drank alcohol and that he'd been too afraid to be honest with him about drinking. He was adamant that he'd gotten sick because he wasn't used to the alcohol. Because of Bill's childhood exposure to his brother's behavior, he was shattered by the familiarity of Adam's denial. Bill wanted to believe it was a one-time occurrence and that Adam would have better judgment in the future.

The Mistake of Wanting to Believe It Isn't True

Adam went on to have two more alcohol-related offenses, which resulted in him having to go before a judge. Judge John Payton in Collin County put him on probation for one year, gave him community service hours, and had Adam report to a probation officer once a month. If Adam was cited with an alcohol- or drug-related offense again before he was eighteen years old, Judge Payton would send him to court-ordered drug treatment. Bill still believed that Adam's problems were isolated and the result of being caught the first time; he believed Adam was unlucky. Barbara believed that Adam lacked life skills because he had been overprotected and raised in an overly sheltered environment. While Bill followed all the rules because of his upbringing, Barbara was afraid that Adam didn't think that the rules applied to him.

It all changed when Bill got permission to take Adam to a family reunion in Mississippi. Because of Adam's probation, he wasn't allowed to go out of the county; however, Bill was able to get permission from the probation officer after explaining that being with family would be good for Adam, especially since his parents were now living apart. Unfortunately, Adam took it as another sign that the rules didn't apply to him.

One night during a family barbecue in his grandparents' backyard in Mississippi, Adam drank too much and passed out in the kitchen where his grandmother found him. Bill could no longer hide the problem, and his family sat down to ask questions about what was going on. Bill was embarrassed, but it was an opportunity for him to see how he was indeed part of Adam's problem. While Adam couldn't be trusted, Bill had continued to act as if he were trustworthy. While Adam needed to live with the consequences of his behavior, Bill continued to campaign for Adam's special treatment. Adam counted on Bill to act as if there was nothing wrong.

At the next marital session, Bill and Barbara gave me the play-by-play of the events in Mississippi. Bill was embarrassed and humbled. Barbara was curiously quiet. She didn't want to rob Bill of his own wisdom. For the first time, I saw Barbara hold back instead of hounding Bill to change his ways with Adam. This created an opportunity for Bill to gain his own wisdom. By the end of the session, Bill believed that he had done his son a disservice by getting him special permission, not holding him accountable, and by believing that Adam had the skills to make good decisions just because he was his son. Bill wanted things to be different for Adam. He had to make a decision.

Bill knew the consequence—Judge Payton might send Adam to a drug treatment center. Bill didn't want him to go. But it wasn't Bill's discomfort about his son being held accountable that was important; Adam had to feel discomfort—maybe for the first time in his life. Barbara wanted to save her son from drug treatment, but believed that if he needed it, he should go. She didn't want to see her son become like his uncles.

Doing the Right Thing

Bill knew the right thing to do: tell the probation officer about Adam's behavior in Mississippi. Bill asked to have a meeting alone with me soon after the marital session. Barbara agreed that it would be beneficial for Bill to talk with me in private.

Originally, Bill had wanted me to see him with his son. I hadn't met Adam, as the focus in Bill and Barbara's therapy needed to be on their marital issues. I asked Bill to come without Adam because I wanted to set the stage for Bill to see that this was an opportunity for him to challenge his own parenting philosophy. I felt that should be done in private, without Adam present.

The probation officer already knew about Adam's offense before Bill's private session—but he hadn't learned about it from Bill. Bill decided Adam should feel some discomfort. He wanted him to feel the kind of growth-oriented discomfort that might help Adam gain his own wisdom. Bill explained to Adam that the probation officer needed to be told. What wasn't negotiable was that the probation officer would know. What was negotiable was whether Bill or Adam told him. Bill set up severe consequences if Adam chose to have his dad tell the probation officer. If Adam confessed, the consequences were less severe. Bill hoped he was giving his son the incentive to do the right thing, the ethical thing, rather than being forced to do it.

Providing the Gift of Life Skills and Ethical, Responsible Judgment

Bill informed me that the probation officer would have to report Adam's offense to the judge. Bill and Adam would find out in the next week if Adam would be sent to drug treatment. At our session, Bill needed a lot of support to convince him that he was doing the right thing. He realized that he had been part of the problem, because he'd wanted to save his son from the kind of life he'd had. In an effort to give Adam what he hadn't had, he forgot to give him what he did have—the opportunity to develop life skills and ethical, responsible judgment.

Chapter Two
SMART Moves:

- Most parents want the best for their children, but spoiling a child may rob them of the ability to gain his or her own wisdom.

- A spoiled and sheltered child may be hindered in developing the ability to function successfully as an adult.

- Do the right thing and don't protect your children from facing the consequences of their behavior. This gives them the opportunity to develop the life skills and the ethical judgment that they need to thrive as an adult.

- Creating an environment conducive to change may breed discomfort. When a child feels discomfort, it is possible that they are more likely to develop an internal incentive to change.

Chapter 3

Did You Think Your Marriage
Would Get Better
When You Had a Child?

Commercials make it look mostly blissful: a baby comes into your life, and you get a five-point Century car seat, the most absorbent (i.e., expensive) diapers, the type of formula that stimulates brain growth, and a new SUV. In the commercials, couples are smiling from ear to ear, they look well rested, and they don't have any reason to argue. (Yeah, right!)

The Change in Satisfaction

For better or worse, marital satisfaction goes down after having a baby. A new parent's world can get pretty chaotic. You really find out what you are made of and how strong your marriage is once you become parents.

What are the typical problems in any marriage? Fighting, emotional distance, lack of trust, and poor communication (to name a few). Your admiration for your spouse can fade for many reasons after having children. These reasons could include:

- Difficulty shifting your identity as a couple to that of a mom and a dad
- The tendency to take each other for granted
- The temptation to simply coexist while trying to get everything done during the day

You both get tired. According to Arlene Jacobs, M.D., specializing in Obstetrics, Gynecology, and Infertility:

> There is always too much to do and your identity as a couple can fade. It is not uncommon for women in the postpartum period to avoid intercourse. Whether it's part self-esteem and getting her body back to an attractive physical being; it is more likely related to the fatigue. It takes energy and the ability to relax to really enjoy and participate in a sexual experience. After a long day of feeding, diapering, not to mention taking care of other children, pack on the chores, the possibility of outside work, the first thing a woman thinks about when she finally gets into bed is sleep or a little private time to relax. Thirty minutes of sex versus thirty minutes of sleep is not a hard decision for most postpartum women. Sexual frequency

is low during the first six months but clearly can improve when the responsibilities and time demands lessen but if this issue lasts longer than six months, it probably reflects deeper issues and should be investigated.

Couples who seek therapy tend to wait an average of six years after they have significant marital dissatisfaction before they come to their first appointment. By the time couples reach an impasse, their problems tend to involve sex, money, work, and childrearing practices. If the divorce statistics are right, and approximately 50 percent of couples will divorce within seven years, what are the 50 percent who remain married doing that's so different?

Are You Scared Yet?

There are some ways to safeguard yourself from the dip in how you might feel about your marriage. John Gottman, Ph.D., has studied marriage for over twenty-six years. He believes he can predict which couples will divorce with over 87-percent accuracy. Two of his books, *Why Marriages Succeed or Fail* and *The Seven Principles for Making Marriage Work*, clearly define the elements of a successful marriage. With his most current research, Dr. Gottman describes the phenomenon of a "relationship meltdown" after a baby is born as a national problem.

According to Dr. Gottman, about 3.6 million babies are born to couples every year in our country. "Right now hospitals prepare couples for only one day in the baby's life, the day of delivery. After that, the couple is on their own. In our longitudinal study of newlyweds, we discovered that two-thirds of couples experience a serious drop in their relationship's happiness in the first three years after the first baby arrives. They also experience postpartum depression at a high rate, and their ability to parent is seriously compromised."

For many of these couples, Dr. Gottman believes that the arrival of the first baby begins a cascade of relationship meltdowns that can lead toward the family's breakup. "All of these events potentially have very serious consequences for the emotional and cognitive development of babies. So, the majority of new families in the U.S. are facing a potential tragedy of major proportions, the unhappiness and/or separation of a baby's parents soon after that child arrives." This tragedy affects the emotional health of the majority of the children in our country.

Attorneys, unfortunately, are the individuals who hear the stories about how marital satisfaction can change to the extreme once a couple has a child.

Lisa Marquis, a Dallas-area family law attorney, offers these observations:
I have met with many prospective divorce clients who report that their marriage changed significantly after the child or children were born. Many fathers come to me stating that the marriage effectively ended after the children were born because their wife put all of her energy into taking care of the children and neglected him and the relationship. I have met with many mothers who feel that even after the divorce, the father of their children should support them to the level that allows her to continue to stay home with the children. Many of these same mothers, however, also complain that their husbands work too much and are not around enough to help with the children. And I have met with many new mothers whose husbands left the marriage shortly after the first child was born because it simply was not what they had expected. Unfortunately, the ones who suffer the most in each of these situations are the ones who never had a say in the matter—the children.

So what can be done about it?

Creating an Opportunity for Change

Having a child can actually create an opportunity for change in a couple. Even if the couple is not experiencing significant difficulties prior to having a child, maintaining realistic expectations about how a marriage will change may be the best way to be immune to the hardships.

It is worth considering that some hardships may not always break a relationship. With appropriate attention and energy, a hardship could actually create an opportunity for change. There is something truly inspiring about couples who go through significant change in their marriage and survive it. Significant change can be anything, not just having a child. The change can be with retirement, the youngest child leaving for college, financial crises, job changes, becoming a caretaker for elderly parents, or the death of a parent. Change could also include moving from one house to another, children growing up, changes in health, and trying to make a decision about whether or not to stay home with the kids.

When I work with couples who have had significant marital stress and low satisfaction for a long time, I hear stories about many of the scenarios I just mentioned. It seems that marital difficulties were brewing and then some event, no matter how insignificant it seemed, appeared to send them into a cascade of marital stress. When they talk about the various events that have caused them to be unhappy, it's as though it just happened yesterday. They have considerable difficulty getting past it, especially if they have neglected to give their relationship the proper attention and energy to be "better for the hardship."

Research on Marital Satisfaction and Birth of a First Child

According to Dr. Gottman and Alyson Fearnley Shapiro at the University of Washington, the prescription for strengthening the marital bond after having a first child is:

- Building fondness and affection for your partner
- Being aware of what is going on in your spouse's life and being responsive to it
- Approaching problems as something you and your partner can control and solve together as a couple

In my clinical practice, I see a number of additional characteristics present in those couples who seem to have become stronger by surviving the stress felt in a marriage. There are a few distinct things that some couples do to ensure that the stress of having a child actually becomes an opportunity for change, rather than one of those events that leads to a cascade of unhappiness.

Being Positively Influenced by Your Spouse

First, couples who manage the stress of a relationship well tend to allow themselves to be positively influenced by their spouse. Additional research by Dr. Gottman actually proves that very low satisfaction in a marriage can be, at least in part, caused by a man's refusal to accept influence from his wife, often due to a fear of losing control. This can result in his emotional withdrawal, or a tendency to try and gain control for himself with defensiveness and contempt, or even with belligerence or domination. That does not mean that men who allow themselves to be influenced are "pansies" or that their wives have more power in the relationship. What it means, especially for couples in the process of having children, is that the couple is able to shift power both ways as they negotiate the change to parenthood.

Regulating Emotions Well

Another characteristic of successful couples is that they tend to know how to regulate their emotions. When they get upset or "put off" by their spouse, they tend to take care of their emotions in a healthy way. This does not mean that they blow it off or walk away from the argument. In fact, I believe that couples who tend to try and blow it off actually tend to recycle the argument for later. Have you ever had an argument where the other person brings something up for the first time, even though the event in question happened a long time ago? Most people can't just blow it off when they get upset.

It is important for both partners in a couple to know how to self-soothe. That sounds weird, but if you think about it, it means that each person is in charge of his or her own emotions. No one can make you feel mad. You decide to feel mad. So when a person feels mad, it is up to him or her to regulate it. It is up to the person to get him or herself under control so that the conversation continues without emotions getting the best of you. It is not a productive excuse to say that you said something out of anger or that you were so mad that you just wanted to hurt your spouse's feelings. Once something is said, it is said, and it is difficult to take it back. The only option left is to get past it.

Maintaining a Level of Satisfaction in Your Relationship Despite Your Differences

Another thing successful couples do to help them have the best relationship possible is staying committed to the goal of having a good relationship. When there are differences of opinion or feelings get hurt, it is important to always stay wedded to the goal of having the best relationship. This doesn't mean that you give up, compromise, negotiate your needs or any of the other ideas you might hear from experts on TV. What it means is that you ask yourself, "What is best for the relationship?"

I believe that the identity of marriage is its own entity. If you listen to the traditional marriage vows, the word "honor" is used. I am not someone who believes that people can only truly feel fulfilled by being in a marriage. There are plenty of single people out there who will argue that they are fulfilled and satisfied in life. But for those of us that have made the commitment to besad married and raise a family, I do believe that the commitment of marriage occasionally requires that things be done a certain way for the sake of the marriage or the family. This is a very delicate balance, because it is often difficult to juggle work and family life. Of course, this is not to suggest that giving to your marriage or your family should be at the expense of each individual involved.

Couples who tend to experience the best relationships know when to put the needs of their relationship first. Let's use the example of allowance. My husband and I have disagreed in the past about whether or not our children should receive an allowance. Because of what I do for a living, I can present him with the research that proves there are successful ways to institute an allowance system, and ways that it can backfire and actually give children the impression that they should get "something" for doing a chore around the house. If parents don't watch out, they may be raising their children to expect a tangible reward every time they are asked to help out. If you ask your sixteen-year-old son to mow the lawn and he says, "What are you going to give me?" maybe the allowance system you use isn't working.

I was raised with an allowance. My husband was raised with a budget rather than an allowance. He felt very passionate about giving our children an allowance for doing their basic chores around the house at an early age. I was not at all on board with this. I believed they should do their basic chores no matter what and additional chores would be extra and could possibly be tied to an allowance system. The conversation started off looking just like an argument. As it progressed, I realized that I was not going to persuade him to see the five hundred reasons why I thought he was wrong. Instead, I took the approach of respecting him and the fact that he felt passionately about giving the boys an allowance. By giving him this respect, I didn't have to agree in order for him to institute it as he saw fit. The more we talked about it, the more I stopped trying to convince him of how wrong I thought he was. Instead, I agreed to support this system without having to institute it myself. In other words, our children had an allowance, but it was only administered by my husband. By doing it this way, I put our marital relationship ahead of my opinions about how an allowance can be successfully instituted. I also allowed myself to be influenced by his opinions without compromising what I believed. This example also shows another skill: understanding the difference between content and process in a marital argument.

Content versus Process

As I work with couples, I notice that those who learn the difference between content and process tend to sustain their ability to have a good relationship. In fact, learning this skill may keep people from needing to go to therapy. As a psychologist, I believe it is my job to work myself out of a job, especially with couples who come in for marital therapy. If I create a situation where a couple becomes dependent on me to solve their problems, then I have done them the greatest disservice. Instead, my focus is always to try and help them get skills and initial relief from whatever caused them to come to therapy, so they leave feeling somewhat hopeful. I want them to have relief even if the problem isn't actually resolved. In therapy, I work to help them discern the process or model they are following, and to see how that approach is causing them to feel unhappy in the relationship. Then I work as hard as I can to teach them how to ask and answer those questions for themselves.

Once most couples understand how to be their own therapist, they will need me less and less because they can do it on their own. They learn to address the process of the argument rather than the content. Content changes frequently. They could fight about money, sex, disciplining their children, work hours, etc. No matter what they disagree about, their model or process will stay the same. By focusing on repairing the model, every type of content benefits in the long run. Believe me: my job isn't to help resolve issues; it's to help a couple develop a healthier philosophy and model of relationships and learn new behaviors to cope with the daily difficulties in life.

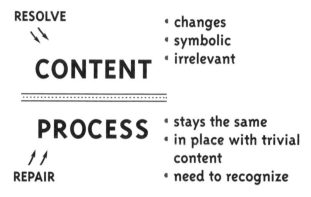

Most people tend to get stuck on content. Let's return to my earlier example about allowance. If I had continued to argue with my husband about all the ways allowance can be instituted inappropriately, I would have been chattering about content, content, content. It wasn't until I stopped with all the ammunition against allowance for basic chores, that I actually began to think in terms of process. Process is the "take a step back and look at what is going on" part of the conversation or argument.

As a marital therapist, I typically find that the role I take is to help people stop the content and step back and look at the process. Instead of thinking, "I am going to convince him that his way of instituting an allowance is wrong and here is why," I was able to step back and tell myself that he was passionate about this. I respected him enough to believe that it was possible for him to potentially motivate the kids to work for their own internal needs and for the external reinforcement of an allowance without my support. Out of respect for him, I stopped with the five hundred reasons it wouldn't work and we instead talked about how I respected him enough to trust that he could do the allowance thing without needing my support. That is the process of the argument.

For couples who tend to have the same argument over and over, it is usually because they keep adding reasons (content) and don't shift their thinking and communicate in a way that is best for the relationship (process). A good metaphor would be what people do when they practice for a play. The actual acting out of the script would be the content, and the decision making and evaluation of whether the scene was flowing correctly would be the process. If couples are trying to create an environment where each person is in charge of regulating their own emotions, then moving to process would help emotions remain in control.

Resolve versus Repair

Finally, many couples come to therapy because they can't resolve an argument. Maybe this is because some arguments are irresolvable. In a marriage there are two different human beings, and it is very likely that one person will see things differently. In fact, I believe it even benefits your children for each parent to have different ways of seeing things. Some day, they will have to get along with all kinds of people—classmates, teachers, and bosses—so, having two parents who have different styles might not be a bad thing. When parents see things differently, maybe it is better to try and repair the relationship rather than resolve the issue. Repairing the relationship involves making attempts to acknowledge the differences and exist in a satisfactory way, rather than get the other person to see your point of view at the expense of the relationship.

Chapter Three
SMART Moves:

- Realize that your marriage will change after the birth of your child.

- View this change as an opportunity and take steps to keep the satisfaction level high in your marriage, despite your differences.

- Remember the difference between content and process: instead of focusing on the reasons in an argument, focus on the ways to communicate that are best for the relationship.

- Some arguments are irresolvable, so concentrate on ways to repair the relationship instead.

Chapter 4

When Life Changes
after Having Children

Everyone has said it: "I won't let having a child change my life." Some people think adapting their lifestyle after having a child is something to avoid. The truth is that we have no idea how our lives will change for the better.

You Don't Know What You Don't Know

Soon after my husband and I were married, we lived next door to the Bressons. For about three years, we were known as "the couple waiting until she got out of graduate school to have children." The Bressons were a family with three children, and as my husband and I went about our daily lives, we noticed that the Bressons were always busy. They were good friends and neighbors, and we enjoyed getting to know their children Jessica, Kevin, and Renee.

The Bressons had a cabin at Holly Lake Ranch in East Texas, and would go there on the weekends until their children became more involved in sports and started having social commitments of their own. They found it more difficult to get away for the weekend because there was so much competition for their time and for the children's time. Before we had children of our own, our conversations with the Bressons were about many things. We talked about events going on in our lives and in the lives of their children. I'll never forget when six-year-old Kevin tried to sell us a rock from our own front yard. We really enjoyed our interactions with the Bresson family. They made having children look easy.

After I got pregnant with our first son, Alex, our conversations started to change a bit. John Bresson would tease us about how our lives would be over. He was always joking, though; it was obvious that John liked being a father. But I know now that John knew what we didn't know, and he was enjoying every bit of the metamorphosis we were about to go through.

One night, when I was a little over halfway through the pregnancy and Mark and I were beginning to buy things for the baby and looking seriously at our childcare options, I went to bed early, as I had another long day ahead of me at work the following Saturday morning. My husband stayed up to watch TV since he could sleep in. He had been working on the computer for a week, filling an Excel spreadsheet with our anticipated expenses once the baby came along. He was obviously stressed and concerned, recognizing that we would have to be very cautious about our future purchases and how we managed our lives. The impending change in our lives was starting to sink in.

For some reason, I woke up at about two in the morning. Mark wasn't in bed, which was strange because he typically didn't stay up that late, even on a Friday night. As I made my first of many nighttime trips to the bathroom, I noticed that the lights were still on in the kitchen and living room. I figured that he was up working on the spreadsheet. I went back to bed.

As I lay there all I could hear was silence. Typically, I would hear the tapping of his fingers on the keyboard. (He can be loud when he is crunching numbers.) I listened and still didn't hear him. I went to investigate, but he was nowhere in sight. His car was in the driveway, so I knew he wasn't far, but I started to feel very nervous all the same. From the back of the house, I could hear noises coming from the Bressons' back yard. I stepped outside and then I could hear John and his wife, Connie, talking about childcare. John had his familiar tone. He is a great storyteller and I could tell from his manner that he was ragging someone. I knew it was my husband, Mark.

As I stumbled through their back gate and came around the corner, Connie and John saw me and started to laugh. Mark was in the hot tub, drinking a Stroh's beer from John's supply. I looked at him and could tell that it wasn't his first of the night. John and Connie gave me a quick synopsis of their conversation with Mark up to that point. I knew what they had been discussing had put him on edge.

There are so many things you think you have to prepare for before you have your first child. There are also many things you don't know to consider until the need presents itself. That night Mark and I found out how much a sitter costs per hour, how many diapers a day a newborn uses, and we got a better understanding of the cost involved with using formula instead of breast feeding. We also got a dose of reality, thanks to the Bressons, because we were introduced to how all those costs become increasingly complicated once you have another child. Little did we know that the Bressons' orientation to having three children would be so valuable once we ourselves went on to have three. We were already too shell-shocked by the ins and outs of the responsibility and costs of having just one. Facing the expenses of three children would have been too much to take at the time.

Having a first child is definitely a turning point. But haven't you ever wondered if men and women see it differently? One study in the *Journal of Adult Development* indicated that women regarded parenthood, the health problems of people close to them, and moving to another community as turning points more often than men. In the same study, men regarded occupational events, military service, and changes in their lifestyle as turning points more often than women. When asked about the most important turning points in their lives, individuals in the study tended to mention points over which they had a large amount of choice. This led to the conclusion that the more personal choice the participants had enjoyed at the time of the turning point, the more positively they evaluated it at the time and later on, in retrospect. This gives us something to think about.

The Biggest Jump Is from Zero to One

People ask me if going from two to three children was tough. There are jokes about when your children outnumber you, and how parenting just gets that much tougher. In reality, my personal as well as clinical experience proves that the biggest jump is from zero to one.

The period surrounding the birth of a child is often one of the most challenging and stressful transitions a couple will experience in their whole marital lifetime. Some couples will be able to experience this change in a way that ultimately enhances personal and marital well-being. For the most part, all couples have some exposure to a decline in marital satisfaction and an increases in personal problems in the months right after childbirth.

Women especially find difficulties because they are dealing with the pregnancy, childbirth, childcare issues, and for many, career-related stressors. Research also found that women tend to report fewer positive feelings about their husbands during the postpartum period than during pregnancy. Further, women report doing much more of the housework and childcare than they had expected. Violated expectations concerning division of labor were related to negative postpartum feelings concerning some aspects of the marital relationship.

Despite any differences related to gender, the changes associated with having your first child are better navigated with a higher level of paternal involvement, especially in caregiving. Research proves that the husband's involvement was associated with a more limited decline in marital satisfaction. In fact, most research suggests that the shared division of labor and responsibilities is particularly important for the maintenance of ongoing marital satisfaction.

Daily Parenting Hassles

What about the hassles of parenting? Keith Crnic, Ph.D., head of the Department of Psychology at Penn State does research on parenting. He describes "daily parenting hassles" as routine caregiving and child-rearing responsibilities that parents may find irritating, frustrating, annoying, and distressing. In his research, he found that high levels of daily parenting hassles relate to lower levels of life satisfaction, frequent negative moods, and increased maternal distress. Daily parenting hassles have been found to be even more stressful to parents than major life events. It is also known that the availability of a social support network can moderate the effects of stress in parenting.

Another aspect of your life that changes once you become a parent is that, for many parents, the child tends to drive the parent to parent interaction. Because we all have different parenting styles, see things differently, and handle situations in different ways, when it comes to interactions that involve our kids, we may react differently. Our kids are watching, so we have to remember and ask ourselves, what are we teaching them?

Continuing to Be Kind: Your Kids Are Watching

This sounds like such a basic thing, but it is so important and necessary that it is worth mentioning. Recently, I was in a McDonald's with my three boys. I was watching them play in the indoor play area. It was a bad weather day, so they were really having a good time. There were two other families that we didn't know in the play area with us. One of the families had a young boy and a girl. The other family was a mother and her two young daughters.

At first the kids were all playing very well together. Then the other boy started spitting on the two young girls. I noticed it, and the mother of the two girls noticed it. We made eye contact—the kind parents make that says, "Do you see what I see? Be on alert." We waited for the other parents to do something, but they didn't. They noticed it, but looked away and kept on eating. When the two young girls nicely asked the young boy to stop, he kept spitting. My boys were unaware of what was going on, and I was secretly hoping they would stay where they were, out of the mess. This whole time, the boy's parents saw and heard what was going on, and still they ignored it. When the young girls were unsuccessful in getting him to stop, their mother stepped in. With a nice, respectful demeanor, she asked the boy to stop spitting and she told her daughters to go to the other side of the area to play on their own. That's when the parents of the spitter started to take note.

This confrontation escalated so quickly that I couldn't even believe it was happening. Little did they know that a psychologist was watching—one who was very aware of how quickly this boy's parents turned ugly. The girls' mother had given the boy the benefit of the doubt; she'd been nice to him and praised her daughters for trying to take care of it themselves. Meanwhile, the parents of the offender watched the whole thing. The mother of the offender began to berate the girls' mother, telling her vindictively, "I will discipline my son if he needs it." She went on to say that her son was just a kid and didn't know any better. Later, she slipped and said her son was five years old. (My professional opinion is that a five-year-old should know better.) The altercation escalated. The offender's parents spewed so much profanity at the other mother that it was astonishing. They were not at a loss for words, and I just waited to see if the McDonald's police would come to our rescue. I just hoped that my kids had their heads far enough in the tubes that they couldn't hear. Finally, the family of spitters left, and we sat there looking at each other. The mother was so shaken that she called her husband to come and make sure the family wasn't going to slash her tires.

Policing Yourself Rather Than Monitoring the Response of Others

We all have these kinds of stories. There are a lot of reasons why tempers escalate so quickly. After September 11, I have seen more people in my practice for anger management than ever before. Privately, I'm hoping it is because people don't want to walk around in a heightened state of aggravation all the time, not that more people are having anger problems.

The man and woman in the McDonald's, however, really took it to the limit. First, what they taught their son was that you can bully people. I also feel a little sorry for his wife. If she makes one mistake, I bet he is all over her. Second, they weren't kind. Even if you disagree with someone, you can be kind about it. They didn't have loyalty to any of the onlookers, but they certainly didn't give anyone the benefit of the doubt. We can use a little kindness. I recently heard from the Centers for Disease Control and Prevention that kindness is infectious. Too bad this man was apparently immune.

Police yourself and ask if you tend to be a hot reactor. Do your conversations begin harshly? Could you benefit from keeping the anger down when something you feel passionate about is in front of you? Having kids has given me a higher level of passion than I have ever felt before. It's amazing what you will do for the sake of your kids. Still, for the sake of our children, shouldn't we all role model control and kindness more often?

Here's an example of missing an opportunity to be kind:
Dad: "What were you thinking? I told you not to eat in the living room. Look what you did. I can't believe it."

Son: "I'll pick it up. You don't have to yell. You are so negative about everything."

Dad: "I just can't believe you did that when I told you not to."

Son: "I said I would clean it up. Don't you have anything nice to say? Stop yelling."

Dad: "I'm not yelling!"

A better way:

> *Dad*: "What were you thinking? I told you not to eat in the living room. Look what you did. I can't believe it."

> *Son*: "I'll pick it up. You don't have to yell. You are so negative about everything."

> *Dad*: "Let me know when you have picked it up, and please be careful next time."

> *Son*: "Okay."

Resisting the Urge to Make Yourself Less of a Priority

As the flight attendants say, if you are on an airplane that loses cabin pressure and you are traveling with small children, put your mask on first and then put your children's masks on them. If you don't take care of yourself, then you can't take care of your children.

On the ground, this also proves true. A lot of women and men come into therapy "hooked into" what is going on with their children. Mothers are busy coordinating car pools, taking their kids to piano lessons, and running to soccer games. Their lives are no longer their own. Dads seem to be coaching this and that, working around the house to fix things, or helping with homework at all hours of the night. If parents work, they come home exhausted, make dinner, try to do the best they can by their kids, then go to bed and start over the next morning.

Sound familiar? We forget to make ourselves a priority, and then we catch ourselves getting angry because other people don't consider our needs.

We Teach People How to Treat Us

If we make ourselves less of a priority, then we risk the possibility that we will train others to treat us poorly. That includes your spouse, as well as your children. If you tell your children they can eat off your plate, they will eat off your plate even when you don't want them to. If you stop what you are doing to get your children something to drink, they will expect it and be upset when you don't accommodate them so quickly in the future. If you stop what you are doing so you can help your spouse at the expense of yourself, then your spouse will expect it, too. Take a second and think about it. If you are concerned that you are being taken for granted by the people around you, ask yourself if you are contributing to the problem.

I am not advocating arrogance. I *am* advocating, however, that you show yourself respect, so that those around you will know you deserve respect. If you are picking your teenager up from a school activity but are pressed for time because of another obligation, train your son or daughter to realize that you might be a few minutes late. If your son or daughter needs to find another ride home rather than wait for you, then they will. Don't allow your teenager to think that his or her needs are more important than yours.

Having a family means you have a lot to do. Before we had our first child, I used to wonder why the Bressons' kitchen light was always on when we got home after a late night out. Now I know. Sometimes they were doing laundry. Sometimes they were watching a movie together. They were fitting it all in and doing what they needed to do to keep their lives the way they wanted while raising three kids. Teaching people how to treat us is not only a lesson for parents to learn, but also it is an idea to role model for our children. It will help them socially and in their own parenting relationships, as well.

Chapter Four
SMART Moves:

- The life adjustment after the first child is the most dramatic.

- Even though the daily hassles of parenting will try your patience, continue to be kind in front of your children.

- Remember to role model the values of control and kindness.

- Respect yourself so your family respects each other.

Chapter 5

Losing Your Cool
with Your Kids

Many parents are surprised by how their own kids can push them to the limit. So many well-educated, resourceful people comment that they feel much more effective in their jobs than they do at home parenting their own children. Maybe the expectations we have for ourselves shatter when someone we gave birth to brings out our extreme frustration.

I'll never forget the night when one of our children cried for what seemed like hours. He was only four months old, and my husband got up to releave me and try and calm him down so I could sleep. It was hard to sleep with our baby screaming. I walked through the doorway to see my husband holding our bundle of joy, looking at him eye to eye, saying, "Just tell me what's wrong!" Of course, if our son had answered back, I would have figured I was dreaming. Instead, it was a typical scenario many parents have experienced, losing their cool over a challenge of parenthood.

Hugging the Tree

One way to monitor your own success in relationships is something I call "hugging the tree." I learned this when I worked with Phil McGraw, Ph.D., otherwise known as Dr. Phil. When Phil prepares an expert witness for the stand, he has them practice what they will say over and over. Now, Phil doesn't tell them what to say, just like I'm not telling you what to say. Instead, he teaches them to stay on task and not to get sucked into discussing nonessential or peripheral matters.

Hugging the tree means staying focused and on task in conversations, especially arguments. Think of the most primitive drawing of a tree. There's the trunk and a bunch of branches. The trunk represents the topic, and the branches represent other tangents.

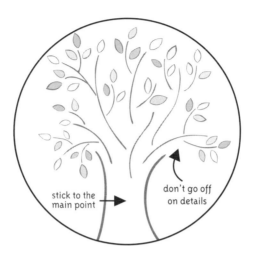

stick to the
main point

don't go off
on details

*This is what it looks like when a dad gets stuck in the branches with his
teenager:*

    Son: "Can I go out tonight with my friends? We want to go to a
movie, but it doesn't end until past my curfew. Is that okay?"

    Dad: "I have confidence you can find something else to do that
would get you home on time. You need to be in by curfew."

    Son: "Dad, don't you trust me? I can't believe it. I've done all my
chores, and I don't have school tomorrow. I don't have to get up early
or anything."

    Dad: "It doesn't matter whether you have to get up early. I said no."

    Son: "You let Sara go out past curfew last weekend. How come she
gets to and I don't?"

    Dad: "Sara is older than you are. She is also more responsible."

    Son: "What do you mean responsible? She's the one that you yell at
all the time for having her music too loud! You yell at her more than
me!"

Dad: "Well, at least she listens when I yell at her."

Son (yelling): "No, she doesn't! She just ignores you."

Dad: "You are so disrespectful. I've told you not to yell."

Son: "Look who's talking!"

Notice how quickly this conversation got off the topic of curfew. When did the dad get swept up in the branches instead of hugging the tree? He started out pretty well by saying his son needed to be home by curfew, but after that, he lost it. Together they went off on tangents about Sara, yelling, disrespect, and fairness. I suspect the rest of the conversation had the father ineffectively perched on the farthest limb like a cat waiting for the fire department.

Are You Teaching Your Child to Argue?

Hugging the tree means staying with the main point. The previous example is pretty typical. Teenagers want you to crawl out onto the branches because it benefits them. By the way, if you don't want your children to argue with you, you shouldn't argue with them. Many parents don't realize that they are giving children the opportunity to argue on a silver platter when they have the kind of conversation you just read.

What would it look like if the dad did a better job of hugging the tree?
   Son: "Can I go out tonight with my friends? We want to go out to a movie, but it doesn't end until past my curfew. Is that okay?"

   Dad: "I have confidence you can find something else to do that would get you home on time. You need to be in by curfew."

   Son: "Dad, don't you trust me? I can't believe it. I've done all my chores, and I don't have school tomorrow. I don't have to get up early or anything."

Dad: "Your curfew is midnight, and I expect you to be home by midnight."

Son: "Dad, that is not fair. All my friends don't have to be home until 1:00 a.m. Their parents are letting them stay out long enough to see this movie. You are treating me like a child."

Dad: "I expect you will do what you need to do to get home by your curfew."

Son: "I can't believe I have to tell my friends we can't go because I have to be home early. I can't believe it!"

Dad: "I'll wait up for you and will expect to see you on time."

The son tried very hard to have a conversation about fairness, "stupid" curfews, trust, and his friends' parents, but the dad wouldn't bite. If you consistently hug the tree, your teenager will know in advance that you won't get sidetracked. The time to have conversations about fairness, curfews, trust, and friends' parents is when there isn't any conflict or imminent decision to be made. It is typically very unproductive to have this kind of conversation when you are in the middle of a negotiation. . . especially one that is heated.

There Is No Blood in Your Brain

When these kinds of conversations get emotional, imagine that all of a person's blood is in their heart. They are full of emotion, and there may not be enough blood in their brain to think clearly. We make a mistake when we try to be logical or attempt to reason with someone who is emotional. It is just like an athlete running a marathon; his blood is literally concentrated in his large muscles. It would be a mistake to eat a lot before running, because digestion slows down so that the body can use all of its available energy for the process of running. Likewise, reasoning with an emotional person can be very unproductive, and maybe even a little nauseating.

The rational person may use phrases like "I think that . . ." or "If you think about it . . ." or maybe even "Think of it this way." The emotional person, on the other hand, will say things like "I don't feel like it," or "It makes me so mad that . . ." It is almost like watching a Spanish speaker and an English speaker try to communicate. If you are trying to talk with someone that is emotional, use "emotional" words to communicate with them until they start to use "thinking" words. That is your cue to begin to reason and problem solve. They won't do it until they are ready.

Teaching People How to Treat Us

Another thing about losing your cool as a parent is that your children will learn two things. First, they will learn how to lose their cool. They will miss the opportunity to learn the productive and smart ways to manage emotion. Second, they will learn to adopt behaviors to try and prevent having you blow up at them. By losing our cool with our kids, we teach them how to treat us.

Amanda and Cameron Grizzle are raising two very likeable and enjoyable young girls. When their first daughter Ansley was born, they found that they struggled, as most new parents do, with how to stay on top of situations. By the time their second daughter Emma was born, they had a better grasp on the concept of maintaining control. Amanda says, "One of the first lessons I learned as a new mother was that I had no control. Control is only available to those willing to take it, and my daughter Ansley, at three months, had it all. Ansley would cry and I'd come running."

> "Want a bottle Ansley? No? Can I burp you? How's that? No? You just want me to hold you? Okay. Can I put you down now? No? Okay." 3 hours later . . .

> "Okay Ansley, let's put you in your swing. No? How about a nap? Can I put you down? Can I eat? Can I sleep? Can I cry with you?"—By the time my second daughter, Emma, came around there was no time for that.

It was more like, "Okay, kid, time for a nap . . . there you go, see ya in a couple of hours." Emma was so much easier. Of course Ansley could have been easy, too, had I not let her condition me to do anything she wanted. It was not my proudest moment when I realized I had been so easily played by a 3-month-old. Oh well, at least I learned fairly early in the game, and most of the time, I'm the one in control today.

Now that her children are in second grade and kindergarten, Amanda continues to toe the line. She says, "The other day we were on our way to our first of a series of horse-back-riding lessons about forty minutes outside of town. Ansley and Emma were bored so they started picking on each other and started up with the 'Mom, Ansley said this!' 'Mom, Emma called me that!' Sometimes I fall victim to this and try to help them sort it out. But on this day I was seeing clearly and said, 'What I'm learning from you guys is that this ride is obviously too long, and unless you can find a way to work it out and get along, this will be our first and last horse-back-riding lesson.' They were perfect angels the rest of the way."

Ask yourself if your child is doing any of the following:
- Lying
- Hiding things
- Forgetting to tell you what happened at school
- Staying in her room and avoiding you
- Walking away from you when you are trying to talk to him
- Keeping bad news from you, so that you hear about problems through someone else

These are some ways your child may be adapting to moments when you lose your cool. The best predictor of future behavior is past behavior. If your child knows that you have lost your cool in the past, they are highly motivated to try and avoid that in the future. In a sense, your child is attempting to regulate your behavior. We teach our children how to treat us.

Low-Value SMART Model

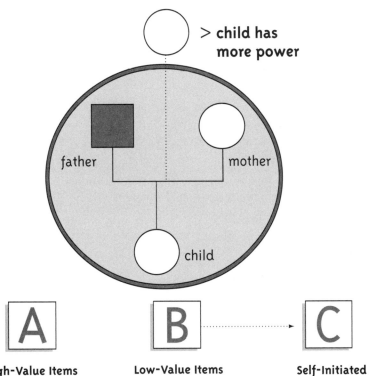

> child has
more power

father   mother

child

| A | B | C |

High-Value Items

- drill sergent
"boot camp"
- opportunity
that matters

Examples:
- get up in a.m.
- go to bed
- friends over

Low-Value Items

missed opportunity
- prompt
- redirect

Examples:
- dishes at table
- carry groceries
- answer phone

Self-Initiated

The smart move would be to control your responses so that your child knows that he or she can be honest and truthful. Manage your emotions, even over the little things; control is possibly more important in terms of the little things. Monitor yourself to make sure you are not "parenting with a hammer" when a little tap will do. I don't mean physically. I mean emotionally. If you lose your cool over spilled cereal, muddy shoes, or when your child forgets his backpack at school with the same emotional intensity that you do with "high-value items," like wrecking the car, then you are in the wrong ballpark. You may actually be inhibiting self-initiated responses. These ideas are part of what I call the Low-Value SMART Model.

The Low-Value SMART Model

The Low-Value SMART Model is actually a way to ensure that parenting can be less work and more effective at the same time. That is a persuasive concept, don't you think? One of my favorite phrases is: "You feed a hungry child a fish a day, and he eats for that day. You teach him how to fish, and he feeds himself for a lifetime." The Low-Value SMART Model is a way to teach your child to feed himself for a lifetime.

One of the mistakes I commonly see parents make is to focus mostly on what I call high-value items.

Examples of high-value items are:
- Wrecking a car
- Failing a class
- Hitting a sibling
- Breaking something valuable

Of course, it is responsible parenting to address high-value items, yet many parents believe that they are ineffective in enforcing change when they focus solely on these items. If this is the case, then I typically begin to look at how they respond to low-value items.

Examples of low-value items include:
- Bringing the groceries in from the car
- Carrying their own backpack into school
- Sharpening their own pencil for homework
- Taking their own dishes to the sink after finishing dinner
- Picking up after themselves

The most telling piece of information for me is how a parent responds to low-value items. Typically, when one parent has a complaint about another parent, it is in response to the high-value items. They say, "My husband yells too much" or "My wife is always grounding our children" or "My husband has a short fuse and loses his cool." The most effective way to improve parenting is to focus more on low-value items.

Here are some points to the model:
- High-value items (A) should be addressed but not at the neglect of low-value items (B).
- Low-value items must be implemented and positively reinforced at least twenty times a day.
- If low-value items are hit more often, then high-value items won't be so out of the blue, and parenting will be more effective.
- Hitting low-value items prepares a child for high-value items.
- After a while, low-value items move into the category of self-initiation, where a child internally decides to do the right thing with little, if any, prompting from you.

Here's what it looks like in real life: If your daughter watches TV while you are cleaning up the dishes after dinner, you are missing the opportunity to hit a low-value item. To get in your twenty times a day, ask your daughter to help bring the dishes into the kitchen from the table before she goes to watch TV. She doesn't have to do all the dishes, especially if she's a five-year-old, but take advantage of age-appropriate low-value item opportunities when they present themselves.

This model:
- Teaches teamwork
- Encourages competence
- Improves self-esteem
- Encourages self-initiation
- Teaches responsibility
- Encourages a child to feel significant and important
- Encourages a child to feel capable
- Institutes good lifelong habits
- Encourages a child to contribute

In considering low-value items, it is also important to not overvalue compliance. Compliance is important and necessary in general. Nevertheless, compliance is more important for high-value items. Expecting total compliance with every low-value item can discourage children from asserting their own needs. It is important to leave room for your child to appropriately bargain and negotiate with you on some of the items. Bargaining and negotiating are skills that need to be role modeled and taught. Even with bargaining and negotiation, parents can still achieve at least twenty successful exchanges of low-value items with their children in a day.

Parents can be open to discussion with their children and allow them to occasionally refuse requests. Children can be taught how to state their case in a logical and persuasive way without having to get unduly angry or upset. Ask questions that encourage children to defend their point of view and learn the appropriate skill that will help them with their peers and as they get older. Of course, parents of very young children will have the advantage, because they will be able to groom their children to the appropriate expectations. Parents of teenagers who already have a history of continual noncompliance may have more difficulty. Still, it can be done with a lot of communication and attention to turn the dynamic around.

The other day, I came home from work and my seven-year-old son, Chase, greeted me at my car. I had a few things to bring in from the car. After we hugged and talked about his day, I asked him to carry in a small bag of office supplies I'd brought home. He carried it in without incident. Because we focus on low-value items in our house, Chase didn't give the task much thought at all. If you follow the Low-Value SMART Model when a child is young, consider what it will lead to when they are adolescents. The parents I work with in my private practice have found that focusing on low-value items, even for adolescents, does wonders for their interaction. It is a parent's responsibility to be attentive to the opportunity that low-value items bring. The payoff is well worth it.

Chapter Five
SMART Moves:

- Don't forget to hug the tree: stay focused and on task.

- Don't be distracted and find yourself stuck in the branches.

- If you don't want your children to argue with you,
  don't argue with them.

- We make a mistake when we try to be logical or attempt
  to reason with someone who is emotional.

- Practice the Low-Value SMART Model instead of focusing
  only on high-value items.

- Implement and reinforce low-value items at least twenty times a
  day. This will increase compliance with high-value items.

Chapter 6

*The Problem with Wanting
to be Friends with Your Child*

We would all prefer that our children like us, and that they want to spend time with us without hesitation. Although most people know that being friends with your child may keep you out of the parenting SMART Zone™, many parents easily make the mistake of being too relaxed when it comes to acting as a parent. They may put being a friend ahead of the role of parent. Without the proper alignment between a parent and a child, trying to be a friend can sabotage your effectiveness as a parent. It can also interfere with judgment of emotional distance, the development of internal resources, and the ability to achieve social competency.

Privacy versus Secrecy

Sometimes you just don't want to know all the facts. Other times, you want your child to tell you everything. Consider how it is with adolescents. If your daughter goes out on a first date with a guy, the conversation she has with you should be different than the conversation she has with her friend. I am not advocating that teenage girls be secretive about what they do, but I do believe that any child or adolescent is entitled to privacy. So how can you tell the difference?

Privacy, according to the *American Heritage Dictionary*, can be defined as "the state of being free from unsanctioned intrusion." Privacy implies something personal that is allowed and not forbidden. Secrecy, on the other hand, implies that there is something possibly harmful, forbidden, or unruly involved. When considering the idea of secrecy, the dictionary includes the concept of concealment and something being hidden, implying the possibility of a malicious intention.

Here are a few examples to help clarify the difference between privacy and secrecy:

Privacy	Secrecy
Age-appropriate coversation about boys	Conversations about inappropriate sex
Discussion about drugs	Discussions about doing drugs
What you think about other people	Gossip that intends to hurt people and is disloyal
Goals and aspirations	Intentions of doing harm to others or self
Asking others to respect your privacy and giving general information rather than specifics	Having to seriously and continuously mislead others to keep a secret

When a parent initially brings a child to see me for therapy, I am very clear about my confidentiality policy. Parents may want to know everything that their child says to me in therapy when they are not in the room, but I always distinguish between privacy and secrecy when I review my confidentiality policy. If a child tells me something they consider private, I will keep the information private as long as it meets my criteria for privacy. I assure the parent and child that I will respect what the child tells me in private; however, if I believe the parent needs to know—in other words, if it really is a secret—I will work with the child to ensure that the parent finds out. If it is a secret, what isn't negotiable is that the parent will find out. What is negotiable, though, is who will tell the parent. The ultimate goal in therapy is for parents and their kids to be able to talk to each other in healthy ways, without the assistance of a therapist. As a psychologist, I am the catalyst for that type of communication. What I have found, is that parents who don't respect privacy typically discover that their child will often withhold important information, leading to many destructive secrets. Many times, that information is something that the parent should know.

When You Don't Want to Know

Then there is the other scenario—you have a child who tells you everything. Sometimes it is about other people, and other times it might be about their own concerns. There are instances when a child can tell a parent too much. Think about the times that one of your kids tells you all the mean things her best friend in third grade did to her during the school day. As you sit on your daughter's bed that night and listen to the pain and agony she felt, all you can think of is how much the other girl betrayed your daughter. You wouldn't mind if your daughter never wanted to see her again. That would please you just fine.

But then it happens: after a couple of days, your daughter makes plans for this girl to spend the night at your house. When she asks your permission, you hesitate because this girl is no longer on your "love list." Apparently, your daughter and this girl have made up. They are now fine with each other and have put the events from earlier in the week behind them. But you haven't, so you aren't sure how to handle the situation. It would be hard to tell if your daughter is setting herself up for heartbreak or if she is on her way to being dumped again. As a parent, you have to somehow distance yourself emotionally, and let your daughter work it out for herself. Reluctantly, you agree to let her spend the night and wish that you didn't know so much about their relationship.

On the flip side, think about what it is like for a child whose parents are having marital difficulties. If a parent discloses too much about their spouse to their child, privacy is not withheld for either the other parent or the child. Even though the child wants to know, the child shouldn't know. It is not about secrets, it's about privacy.

Think about what this looks like later in life, in a similar scenario. Perhaps when your daughter is an adult, you won't want her to tell you all about her marriage when things are tough. It might be too difficult for you to forgive and forget.

Emotional Distance Model

I have developed another model that provides a simple way to evaluate emotional distance in relationships. Emotional distance is the emotional attachment or degree of engagement between two people. Sometimes people have trouble being too attached or engaged. Other times, the problem is that two people may be emotionally detached or disengaged. The Emotional Distance Model is a way to pictorially describe the idea that relationships, without the appropriate emotional distance, tend to be unstable. The general model is shown below.

Emotional Distance Model

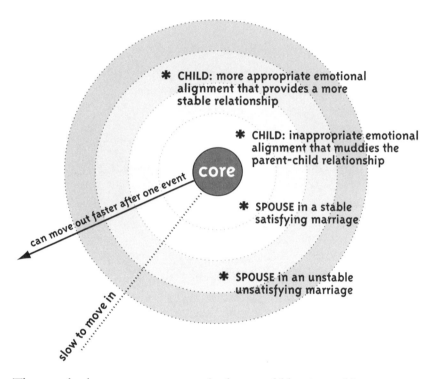

* CHILD: more appropriate emotional alignment that provides a more stable relationship

* CHILD: inappropriate emotional alignment that muddies the parent-child relationship

core

* SPOUSE in a stable satisfying marriage

can move out faster after one event

* SPOUSE in an unstable unsatisfying marriage

slow to move in

The people closest to you are people that would be situated in your core. They are the people you trust most, the ones you rely on for emotional support and the ones who tend to know you best. We would all hope that in our marriages, our spouse is in our core. When that is true, the marriage typically is stable and successful. If there is more emotional distance or disengagement in a marriage, then the spouse would be considered further from the core, almost periferal to what is going on with you emotionally and cognitively you tend to be out of sync.

There are also times that a close relationship doesn't belong in the core. That would be the case for a parent and a child. If we refer to the same model, plotting a child in a parent's emotional core would lend itself to all sorts of problems. The better emotional alignment would be for a child to be in the outer ring of the emotional core.

The consideration of proper parent-child emotional positioning includes many benefits for a child:
- More appropriate boundaries
- Better success with discipline
- Respect for the child's privacy and for the privacy of the adults
- Allows the child to develop social judgment
- Allows the child to develop internal resources

In addition to the parent-child relationships I've described, there are a number of other relationships that illustrate why emotional distance should be considered:
- There may be a perception of trust between two people who are emotionally engaged or attached that hasn't been earned or solidified. For a child, that would be the scenario described previously, where there is the "on again/off again" routine between friends, which over time makes it hard to know where the relationship stands. Poor emotional distance com promises healthy emotional safety
- There may be difficulty feeling in sync, which is created by disengagement that might appear on the surface to be a lack of concern or caring. This would be the case in a marriage where there is instability and dissatisfaction.

For the child who is now an adult, emotional distancing is also an important factor. Take this example: Nancy lives with her husband and three children in Georgia. Her father, Frank, divorced Nancy's mother over fifteen years ago. A short time after the divorce, Nancy's mother passed away. Frank moved to Georgia from California to live closer to Nancy and her family. For the most part, Nancy and her family have felt very fortunate to have Frank in the same city. Nancy's children benefit from having their grandfather so close, and Frank is generally a good influence on Nancy's kids. But, over time, Nancy and Frank's relationship has become strained. Nancy described the relationship with her father:

> Once my parents divorced and my mother passed away, my father began to rely solely upon me and my brother to fulfill his emotional needs. I became his best friend, confidante, the host of birthday parties and holidays for him, his cook, his social encourager, and his advisor. Although I love my dad, by the time I had children of my own, it became draining to be his social security blanket. I was leeched enough from my own children. I started feeling resentful that he relied so much on me and my family. I started distancing myself from my dad, not only for my sanity, but for his benefit as well. If he didn't have me to rely on, then my hope was that he would be forced to create some new emotional relationships on his own.

A parent who becomes too much of a friend may be interfering with the development of SMART internal resources.

Developing SMART Internal Resources

An important component of the development of the parent-child relationship is the ability of a child to develop internal resources versus relying too heavily on external resources for development. Infants rely very heavily on external resources for their every need. Toddlers begin to recognize their "me" identity, but they still need the comfort and reassurance from an external source, most importantly a parent. As children begin to develop autonomy in early childhood and ultimately in adolescence, it is important that internal resources are developed so that a child can learn to self-soothe and problem solve using their own means.

An example of how a parent can help foster independence is to encourage the recognition of their child's own internal ability. One day, I picked our son Chase up from preschool and he was full of excitement; he had a piece of paper in his backpack that he wanted to show me. There on the paper he had written his full name, Chase Fletcher. He was so proud. As I drove with him in the backseat, I told him how proud I was of him—an understandable response for any parent, under the circumstances. Still, that is only an external resource reinforcing him. I wanted Chase to be able to reinforce himself as well. I took the opportunity to strengthen the development of Chase's internal resources by simply saying, "I'm so proud of you; aren't you proud of yourself?"

By giving a child the opportunity to develop his or her internal resource to praise him or herself, we are giving a great gift—the opportunity to develop internal reinforcement.

Soon after that day, my son went one step further. We were doing laundry together, and he took on the task of folding a bedsheet. He had seen me do it a hundred times. I fold a bedsheet by taking it out of the dryer, spreading it out over the dining-room table, and folding it so that I get all the corners matched up and straight. Chase, all on his own, took a bedsheet to the dining-room table and proceeded to fold it with corners straight into a tight bundle that would fit perfectly in the right spot in our linen closet. I hadn't seen him do this. I was too busy moving the laundry from the washer to the dryer. When he was done, he walked up to me with the neatly folded bedsheet lying in his extended arms. "Mommy," he said, "look how I folded this sheet all by myself. I am so proud of myself." He walked away with a confident grin. It was priceless.

Every once in a while we get confirmation that our intentions are paying off. Remember, "Feed a hungry child a fish, he eats for that day; teach him how to fish, and he feeds himself for a lifetime." Chase fed himself that day. Providing an opportunity for the development of internal resources will always be in the best interest of your child.

Examples of SMART ways to provide an opportunity to develop internal versus external resources are:

External	Internal
"Do this for me."	"Do this for yourself."
"Wait until your father gets home."	"Think about how you might make this right."

Social Competency

As a parent continues to develop his or her parenting philosophy, it is important to recognize that children will need our influence as parents in order to develop their own social competency. Social competency exists because of two components: The first is overall group acceptance. Group acceptance is the tendency to be liked by one's peers and feeling part of a group. The second component is made up of friendship. Friendship can be defined as the ability to form and maintain close personal relationships with individual members of the peer group. Here is another reason why being friends with your child may not be in his or her best interest, as social competency is fueled by peer relationships. It would be expected that a parent-child relationship may be more forgiving than a child's relationship with peers.

According to research, both compartments—group acceptance and friendship—contribute in distinct ways to a child's development, including a sense of self-worth, school achievement, general life adjustment, and well-being. According to Hara Estroff Marano, author of *Why Doesn't Anybody Like Me?*, group acceptance and friendship not only reveal, but also further foster a child's social understanding and individual development.

Hara Estroff Marano offers some pointers for parents:
- Know about kids' peer competence, but don't make a career out of it.
- Encourage your children to explore their environment and to enter new situations.
- Regard your children's social life as a necessity, not a luxury.
- Value your children's social play.
- See that your children have unhurried time to play with peers.
- Provide your children access to unstructured activities.
- Utilize quality time with your children as an opportunity to gain valuable social skills.
- Let your children see you interacting with other people.
- Polish your own social skills.

Cathy Evans, Ph.D., was previously employed as a school psychologist for a local school district. Her experience with students and their parents illustrates the importance of taking advantage of opportunities for children to develop social competency and internal resources. Dr. Evans remembers contacting parents about their children being caught cheating, being noncompliant, or being disruptive to other students. Typically, she was asked to contact parents if the teacher had difficulty managing the student's behavior in the classroom. Dr. Evans described the experience:

> It always caught me off guard when parents were so quick to perceive their child's conflict as difficulty between the teacher and their child, or, more commonly, conflict stemming from a "difficult" teacher. When parents viewed the problem as external (difficult teacher) rather than internal (difficulties within their child), it hindered the development of that child's internal resources. It often seemed like a quick solution to change teachers. However, changing teachers does not fix the child. That same child may go to the next teacher in a new environment and present the same exact challenges. The child wouldn't have developed a new internal strategy to take with him or her to the new setting. Parents can view the difficulty as an opportunity for their child to mature. Then internal strategies can have been taught and positive change the more likely outcome.

Now a stay-at-home mom, Dr. Evans eagerly anticipates the birth of her third child, Devin. For the benefit of her own children, she recognizes the importance of aligning her relationship with her children Benjamin (age four) and Paige (age two) early:

> While I want my children to like me and consider me their friend, I know it's more important that I align as a parent. I have to remember that my children really have no idea what is in their best interest. I love my children and want them to love me, too. I even hope that they will like me. But if I can't teach them at home where they feel the most safe (by behaving like a parent), then how can I expect them to learn outside our

house? Quite frankly, most of the time it would just be easier to give in to Benjamin and Paige's demands. Think about it— all the candy they possible want (this would keep them entertained for quite a while), bedtime whenever they want (no temper tantrums about going to bed), no bath (again, elimination of tantrums about taking a bath), all of the television they want (the house would be so quiet), and of course, any toy or candy visible in a store (again, no tantrums). But am I truly making a "friend" by allowing my children to determine what they want? Is it really in their best interest? Sure, short term, they might be excited to indulge in candy; they might think I am the best mom. But in the long term, will I really win by being their friend and having them "like" me? Will they win? I have to remind myself when they are screaming and crying (because I said no to a request) that it will pass.

SMART Moves:

- Learn to distinguish between privacy and secrecy; allow and respect your child's privacy.

- Learn to gauge the emotional distance you should have in certain relationships. According to the Emotional Distance Model, a parent-child relationship should not be in your core.

- Help your child develop internal resources so that they can learn to self-soothe and problem solve using their own means.

- Realize the importance of your child's social play and peer interaction in gaining their own social competencies.

Chapter 7

*When Your Child Doesn't Come to
You When He Needs to Talk*

We all expect our children to come to us when they need to talk. We want it that way, even though we may not want to actually hear what they have to say. We may not like knowing everything, but we at least hope that we will succeed in communicating with our children.

Sometimes it is not that easy. We may see behavior that concerns us. Sometimes behavior communicates even more than the spoken word. In a preschooler, this can be in the form of tantrums. In an adolescent, it may be behavior that signals withdrawal. Even if your child is not using his or her words, they are definitely communicating. Having the kind of relationship where you and your child can communicate involves asking the right questions, setting him up to take responsibilities for his actions, talking about the tough stuff, and helping him take responsibility for the problem.

Why Ask Why?

In terms of communication, one of the most overused questions in the English language is "why?" So many times people will ask someone why they did something, when in fact there is no acceptable answer. A case in point: if you have a person break into your house on Christmas Eve by bashing in a window with their foot, then stealing a big container of change worth about four hundred dollars, and walking out with a few of your eight-year-old son's Christmas gifts, would there be an acceptable answer to the question, "Why did you do that?" I think not. If there really is no acceptable rationale for this behavior, why give the offender the chance to drum up a reason?

Parents waste a valuable opportunity, asking a child "why?" Instead, ask SMART "how" and "what" questions. Here are some examples of the slight changes you can make that may increase the likelihood of improved behavior:

Why Questions	Smart (How & What) Questions
"Why did you hit your brother?"	"How are you going to make it up to him?"
"Why did you take money out of my purse?"	"How are you going to pay back the money you took from my purse?"
"Why didn't you do your chores like I asked you to?"	"What are you going to do to get your chores done on time?"
"Why did you lie about that?"	"What are you going to do to earn our trust?"
"Why didn't you get up on time for school this morning?	"What are you going to do to get up on time tomorrow?"
"Why did you use so many cell phone minutes?	"How are you going to pay for the minutes you used?"

You may have noticed the trend. The "why" questions lead you to a dead end. There are few responses, if any, that you would accept. "How" and "what" questions, however, provide an opportunity for the child to take responsibility for unacceptable behavior and offer an appropriate alternative. It gives the child a chance to make it right. There are a lot of responses to these types of questions that would be acceptable. It also does not usually shame or blame for the behavior. When I review this strategy with parents it makes total sense to them. It also makes them hypersensitive to how the word "why" is overused, when "how" or "what" are far more productive.

Setting Him Up to Be a Better Liar
If you keep asking "why," you will get an answer; of course, the answer may not be truthful. It may be creative. It is possible that there is not an acceptable answer to the "why" question, no matter what the question is about. Are you really communicating well if you ask "why" but are unwilling to accept any of the answers? My guess is that you would be

setting your child up to practice the art of "creative justification" only to shoot her down if you ask "why?" but already know that the behavior was unacceptable and there is no good answer. I would think that for most kids, especially teenagers, if they are given the chance to explain "why," but you still don't accept the answer, it might entice them to get mad and feel as though you are not giving them a chance.

How Behavior Communicates: When No Words Are Needed

There is another dynamic of behavior that is commonly missed by parents. It is not unusual for a parent to tell me a story about how their child misbehaves, describing the misbehavior as a blatant and an obvious cry for attention. They fear that giving too much attention to the misbehavior will possibly reinforce the behavior, making it likely that their child will repeat the conduct in order to get attention. What is it about parents being afraid of giving their child attention for inappropriate behavior? The improper action may actually be the child's way of communicating, and the behavior may actually extinguish if a parent gives attention to it. The behavior may be your child's way of communicating there is a problem, even though your child is not totally aware of what the problem is.

For instance, long before I had children, I had more than one parent tell me how their young child would act like his foot was caught in the cushions of their couch. The first time I heard this I just had to ask what they meant—it sounded so ridiculous. The parents didn't hesitate to show me how their son (although sometimes it was a daughter) would wedge his foot into the crack between the cushions and cry that it was stuck. He would whine until one of his parents came to help him get his foot out of the couch.

Now, most parents would find this scenario ridiculous. They would fear that giving attention to it would reinforce the behavior. They might be afraid that they would actually be rewarding the behavior, and that it would repeat itself if the child thought it worked to get attention. They are afraid that it might feel good to the child to get a response. It is tempting to tell the child, "Oh, you're okay. Get your foot out of the couch yourself. I don't want to hear it anymore." It might be tempting, but it would be a shame to miss the real message in your child's behavior.

If you ask yourself what the purpose of his behavior truly is, you might be able to shift your thinking a bit. You might be able to identify what your child needs, even when your child isn't capable of communicating it with words. It's safe to assume that the foot-in-the-couch behavior communicates an important message. The message is, "I need your attention and I am going to do something to get it. Something so ridiculous that you will have to come over and help me. I will make it sound really bad so you have to give me the attention I crave." What is a better low-risk behavior than a foot caught in the couch? As a parent, would you prefer a child starting a fire, locking you out of the house, or breaking something of value to you?

So what do you do? If your goal is to extinguish the behavior, consider giving him some attention. This may curb the behavior because it may turn out to be so satisfying that he gets his "attention fix" and will be less likely to repeat the behavior. But it is very important that you take the hint. It is possible that he is communicating his feeling that you don't give him enough attention, and he is going to try this "or something like it" to see if he can get you to focus on him.

Now, this has come full circle. Just as I was getting used to hearing parents tell me their child would complain about his foot in the couch, her hand stuck in a jar, his shoe not going on the right way, or her stomach hurting when she woke up in the morning, one of my own children at four years old one day presented the foot-in-the-couch scenario. I couldn't believe it. It was as if he had read a textbook and decided to try and stump me. At first, I felt the urge to say, "Oh, Sam, get your foot out of the cushions. You are okay." Then I came to my senses and realized this was the real thing. I told myself, "Okay, Dr. Know-It-All, now that it's your turn, don't mess up."

I walked over and helped him get his foot out of the couch and then redirected him by saying, "Hey. Do you want to help me check my e-mail? You can sit on my lap, and I'll let you click the mouse to open the messages." Instead of thinking, "If I give him attention, it will reward the behavior, and he will think it is okay to do it again," I thought, "He needs some attention, so I will give him just enough for the foot thing, and then I will redirect him with more appropriate attention."

Before we leave this idea, there is another way we may see this scenario—in a more adult context. When a husband goes out to socialize with his friends, a wife could be concerned that he might drink more than he should. When she begins to nag him, telling him all the reasons he shouldn't go, it is not always her way of trying to control him. It can also be the way she communicates that she is scared and needs to know that he will be okay and responsible.

Another example is when a relative gets on your case for not calling more often. It may sound like they are complaining, but they are really attempting to say, "I miss you and want to hear from you more. When I don't hear from you I worry that something bad has happened to you. Then, when you call and I realize you are okay, I chew you out for upsetting me!" Sometimes it is difficult for them to successfully communicate their feelings. When you sense that this is the case and you believe that the person is not being direct about their needs, it might be more effective to respond to the underlying message. When a wife nags about wanting her husband to stay home, he might want to offer her more reassurance that he will be responsible and she doesn't need to worry. That response would be different—and far more constructive—than simply getting defensive.

When the relative gets on your case about not calling more often, respond by asking, "Has it been that long since we talked? I can't believe it. I miss talking to you, too. Tell me what has been going on? What have I missed?" It would be a real sidetrack to get into a conversation about how busy you are and that you keep meaning to call, but haven't. That would be defensive and would possibly only set you up for more conflict.

We tend to expect adults to communicate more directly, instead of leaving it up to the other person to interpret the behavior or fears. For children, however, it is a little different. Children may not always be in touch with how they feel, and they may not even recognize that their behavior is a safer way for them to communicate, compared to words.

Sex, Drugs, and Rock & Roll, Cell Phones and the Internet

What about communication for the hard subjects? Did you go to your parents for advice about sex and peer pressure? Do you really expect that your children will come to you? I think it is possible, but tread delicately.

Sex

Whether you realize it or not, you are always communicating about sex with your children. You do this when you cover yourself up when your daughter walks in the room while you are dressing, when you watch a television commercial with people kissing each other, and when you and your spouse show affection for one another. There are important things to communicate when it comes to sexuality. According to Elena Love, a Planned Parenthood Executive and a Licensed Professional Counselor:

> We want our children to experience healthy, satisfying, sexually intimate relationships when they are capable physically, emotionally, and circumstantially of managing the consequences of these relationships. Most of us believe that childhood is fraught with enough challenging learning experiences without the addition of premature sexual involvement. With this in mind, it is understandable why we try to shield our young children from sexually explicit behavior in the media and why we often go to great lengths to preserve the privacy of our own intimate behavior. It's a protective instinct. We don't want our children to witness sexual activity, whether real or dramatized, which we fear may inspire them to experiment with these behaviors before they are ready to handle the consequences. We probably know intellectually that seeing mommy naked or watching soap opera stars go at it on TV isn't going to catapult our children into premature sexual experimentation, but on an emotional level we're going to do everything we can to buy time—till we think they are ready to handle the stress of a sexually intimate relationship.

Use things in the natural environment as an opportunity to communicate effectively, in your SMART Zone, about sex. The information should be age appropriate and the rule of thumb is to give general information and respond to questions when they come up. Remember that it is possible to give too much information, talk over their heads, and appear judgmental. The sign across your forehead should read, "I'm happy to talk to you about sexuality, and you can count on me to talk with you honestly."

Drug and Alcohol Use

One of the problems with the subject of alcohol is that your children will be exposed to it at an early age. If they are around other kids, they are exposed to the possibility of substance abuse. That doesn't mean that others are actually doing it in front of them, although sometimes they are. It means that they are going to know about drugs. They will hear many different reasons to use them and many reasons not to. The key to drug prevention is to instill the internal motivation that your children have too much going for them to put their future at risk with drug use. But it isn't simple to implement.

If we include alcohol as part of drug usage, there is another problem. Many first experiences your children will have with alcohol will not be bad. They might be hesitant, but try it anyway. Most children won't puke or get caught drinking the first time. In fact, there may be no negative consequences at all. That is part of the problem. The fear is that they will gain confidence that they can handle it and pursue it further.

I always tell people that I don't want my children to drink alcohol as teenagers, but because my husband and I are raising three children, it is very possible that at least one, if not all three of my kids will try alcohol as a teenager. When they do, I want them to puke their guts out and be sicker than they have ever been, and then I will make them mow the lawn in hundred-degree heat and eat pancakes with syrup. I want them to taste it, touch it, and feel it. It is the principle of classical conditioning. If they go to try it again, I want to evoke the memories of a negative experience so they have a strong aversion to doing it. Remember Pavlov's dog salivating when the bell rang? I want my kids to do the same, but in a way that makes them feel sick, too sick to want to try it again, until they are responsible and of age.

The goal is to allow the environment to promote negative conse-quences so that they won't want to do it again. If they are hungover, don't baby them. If they need to miss school, don't write them a note excusing their absence. If they are using alcohol or other drugs, don't hide it from your spouse. Too often, the negative consequences of drug and alcohol use are not immediate; your children will think they are invincible and that they can handle themselves. If you think your children are experi-menting with drugs, address it immediately and keep tabs on them. If they don't want you to know they are doing something, you won't know until they become sloppy about hiding it. When there is evidence of use, don't dismiss and ignore it.

Rock & Roll

Music is a typical source of arguments for parents and their children, especially when they are teenagers. It is no longer that it is just too loud; now parents are concerned about the lyrics. Music helps us see the dif-ference in the way a parent sees the world and the way their child sees the world—whether it is about their music, choice of clothes, or friends.

If you make a negative remark about the way your child dresses, their choice of friends, or the music they listen to, then you are making a remark to your child about the way you see him or her. They will take it personally. At some point, it might be the way they wear their hair or the way they wear make up. I'm not going to tell you not to express your opinion, but I do encourage you to express your opinion in a way that doesn't give the message, "I don't respect you."

I recently had a mother and daughter in my office fighting over whether or not the daughter's clothes were too revealing. The word the mother used was sleazy. I agreed with her that the daughter's clothes were too suggestive. Unfortunately, her daughter had already been through a full day of school, and no one had sent her home for violating the dress code. She had gone to school that morning wearing an oversized sweat-shirt, hiding her real outfit when she left the house. As soon as she arrived at school, she left the sweatshirt in her locker. By the time they were in my office that afternoon, it seemed to the daughter that her mother was the only one complaining about what she was wearing.

At first, the mother began to lay into her daughter about "what she was advertising" and how others would perceive her. That's when I asked the daughter to go sit in the waiting room, so I could talk to her mother in private. I didn't want to talk to the mom this way in front of her daughter, as the daughter could have perceived it as me giving her permission to dress in such a revealing manner. After letting the mom know how I thought she was viewed by her daughter, I gave her another way to approach the clothing problem. It went something like this:

"I know you really like wearing that outfit, and you think it looks pretty good on you. I'm concerned that it is too revealing and that it shows too much of your body. If you are wondering why people look at you, or why the guys look at parts of your body instead of your face, it might be because you are leaving little to their imagination. If you are going to wear that outfit, save it for when you have friends over, or for times you are outside of school. Wear it with our family around."

When her daughter tells her later that she wants to wear it to school, her mother can ask her to wear it a couple of times to other events that the mother considers safe and where there are others who might be more credible in telling her it is too revealing. The problem is there may be few people willing to say this. Most likely, the daughter will try to wear the outfit again without her mother's knowledge, however, if you create an environment where she grows tired of it, then it is possible that she will decide to make better choices. If you tell her you think she looks awful, you will alienate her for sure and create an environment where she believes you are after her. As a result, she will fight to keep doing what she is doing.

Cell Phones

Cell phones are a luxury that have become for many teenagers a necessity. I have so many families telling stories of huge bills run up by their teenagers on cell phones. There is no argument that everyone sees the benefit of having a cell phone in an emergency. Unfortunately too many teenagers overuse cell phones in the course of their social life. Save them from themselves. Monitor cell phone use, especially minutes before there is a problem. Consider using calling cards to avoid overuse. Having a teenager reimburse you for a $300 cell phone bill could take many weeks of chores. In the real world it is expected that you pay first and use second. We are handicapping our children if we allow them to use first and intend to pay second. Don't wait until there is a problem to monitor minutes. Catch the problem early before the money comes out of your pocket.

The Internet

Children and teenagers are the fastest growing group of internet users. According to the U.S. Department of Justice and ProtectKids.org:

- 75 percent of children are willing to share personal information online about themselves and their family in exchange for goods and services. (eMarketer)
- About 25 percent of the youth who encountered a sexual approach or solicitation told a parent. (Youth Internet Safety Survery)
- One in five U.S. teenagers who regularly log on to the Internet say they have received an unwanted sexual solicitation via the Web. Solicitations were defined as requests to engage in sexual activities or sexual talk, or to give personal sexual information. (Crimes Against Children Research Center)
- Only 25 percent of solicited children were distressed by their encounters and told a parent. (Crimes Against Children Research Center)

It goes without saying that internet use by children and teenagers must be monitored. Many children are using the internet and instant messaging their friends without the supervision of adults. While we can't look over their shoulder all the time, we can put the computer with the internet in a central place in our homes so there is less privacy. Remember when telephones had cords? Growing up, our family only had one phone in the kitchen that was the one we all used. While I was on the phone with my friends I knew at any minute my parents would walk through, without me knowing, and possibly hear what I was talking about with my friends. Today so many parents tell me how their children are up in their rooms, supposedly doing homework when in reality they are chatting and surfing the net. My suggestion is to have computers in your home at workstations that are visible to anyone walking into the room. I also encourage parents to install software to monitor where their children have been. You should even tell your children you are doing so. That is a wild idea but one that is a deterrent. Again, don't wait until you find out that your child is being solicited over the net or visiting websites that are inappropriate to begin pulling the plug. Internet safety precautions are as important as putting training wheels on a bike, having ratings for movies, and keeping your child's bedroom door open when they have friends over. It just makes sense.

Pushing Them toward the Problem

I see another way that parents create an environment where their children are less likely to come to them with a problem. It is when you, as a parent, become part of the problem because you unknowingly push them closer to it. Consider the example of your son having a best friend who often gets into trouble. The more you tell your son that you don't like him hanging around this child, listing all the reasons why, the more vehemently your son will defend his friend. Ultimately, he will convince himself that his friend is pure and right.

Very often, the more you forbid something, the more your child will defend it. The more your child tells you something that you don't believe, the more they will believe it. Here is one way to look at it:

The daughter says, "I'm ugly."

You say, "No you are not."

The daughter says, "Yes I am. All the boys say so."

You say, "They don't know what they are talking about."

Then she proceeds to tell you the fifty reasons why she thinks she is ugly.

You give her the fifty reasons that you are right and she is wrong.

After you give her the fifty reasons why you are right and she is wrong, she walks away from the conversation believing even more doggedly that she is ugly. Meanwhile, you think you made a difference. Here is another way to have the conversation:

> The daughter says, "I'm ugly."

> You say, "Oh honey, that makes my heart hurt to hear that you think you are unattractive. I look at you and see all your beauty both inside and outside. When I hear you say you don't see it yourself, it makes me sad. What's that like? Maybe I can help you see what I see."

Notice that you still have the chance to say that you don't agree with what the boys at school say (and what your daughter has come to believe of herself), but you also create an opportunity for her to talk about how she feels without it being negated. You can create an environment where she has the option to consider what you say, rather than one where she tries to convince you of her argument. If you consider the second option, you are more likely to generate an opportunity where your child can come to you—with both the good and the bad.

SMART Moves:

- Ask SMART "how" and "what" questions. "Why" questions only lead to dead ends.

- Often, children can't communicate with words, so they communicate with actions. Sometimes, disobedient behavior is really a cry for attention.

- Remember the most effective ways to discuss difficult subjects such as sex and drugs.

- Don't push your children toward a problem by becoming part of the problem.

Chapter 8

*How to Tell If Your
Child Has a Problem*

I hope that we all expect our children to be healthy and well-adjusted. When we think of what our children will be like, we imagine that he or she will get only our best physical features. I never had any images of my children having anything but red hair. It didn't matter that only I had red hair, and my husband's was more blackish-brown. It was just the natural look that I thought each of my kids would have. Besides physical characteristics, I also believed that my children would have a love of reading, enjoy calculated risks, and enjoy cutting it up with the best of them. That said, the personalities of your children can challenge you, often making it more difficult to read a situation or relate to their experience in the same way.

Personality (with a Little Temperament and Character Mixed In)

An individual's personality is one of the things that make him or her stand out from other people. Personality is developed and groomed by a variety of experiences and variables, even when it appears that some of the variables are the same. Anyone with more than one child will tell you that each of their children's personalities is distinct, even though they have been raised in the same environment. Then there's this thing called temperament. Temperament is decided before you are born. According to the *Encyclopedia Britannica*, "Temperament is an aspect of personality concerned with emotional dispositions and reactions and their speed and intensity; the term often is used to refer to the prevailing mood or mood pattern of a person."

According to David Keirsey, a major researcher on temperament, there are two sides to personality; one is temperament, and the other, character. He offers that temperament is a configuration of inclinations, while character is a configuration of habits. He further describes character as disposition and temperament as a predisposition.

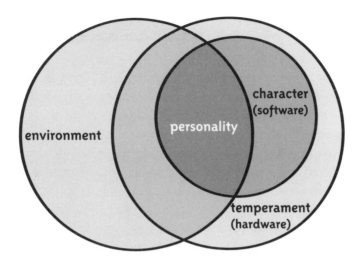

David Keirsey describes our brain as a sort of computer that has temperament for its hardware and character for its software. He believes that the hardware is the physical base from which character emerges. This may explain why the underlying consistency in personality can be observed from a very early age, long before our experience or social context (one's particular software) has had time to influence a person. Therefore, temperament is inborn, and character develops through the interaction of temperament and environment.

Temperament, character, and personality are seemingly inherited and configured just like brown eyes, a broad nose, big ears, and red hair. We might be more accepting of some of the inherited physical features, but temperament, or personality features, is another story. According to David Keirsey, not only are we predisposed to developing certain attitudes and actions and not others, but these actions and attitudes are also unified—they tend to hang together.

Sophie first came in as a patient at the age of seven. She was so cute. She had brown hair that could be styled in a ponytail, worn straight down, or curled to look natural and easy. She was very curious at the start, and is one of the only children I've seen walk behind my desk, open my drawers, and look for gum. Her mother, Merryll, was fast on her feet and reached for Sophie's hand before the gum went in her mouth.

Sophie's parents brought her in because she was having difficulty getting along with other children in her class. The teacher told her parents that Sophie was interfering with the other children's ability to learn while in the classroom. Sophie's parents were also having difficulty with the place where Sophie was staying for after-school care.

Sophie was in the first grade, and her parents thought starting school would have been the turning point for her to begin experiencing more success. Merryll was an attorney and Sophie's father, Tim, was a very successful professor at the local university. Both parents were high achievers with extensive vocabularies. They were very sincere when they talked about their love for their daughter. They were just as honest when they talked about how bad some days with Sophie could be.

Days earlier, before meeting Sophie, I had an appointment with her parents to hear about her history and get a good idea of their greatest concerns. Even with two graduate degrees, I still have to concentrate on maintaining good customer service skills; and even though Sophie was the patient, Merryll and Tim were the real customers. Sophie's disruptive symptoms were more disruptive to Tim and Merryll than they ever were to Sophie.

The first thing Tim and Merryll told me was that Merryll had a very easy pregnancy and an uneventful birth. Sophie was the first of two children. Her brother Steve was born two years after her. He was now five years old. Soon after Sophie was born, Tim and Merryll noticed that she had a greatly exaggerated startle reflex. When there were sudden noises or movements around her, she tended to startle in an overblown manner and cry for extended periods of time.

Sophie had always been very difficult to soothe. Tim told stories of driving around town for hours with Sophie in her car seat, trying to get her to calm down and go to sleep. Tim had even been questioned by the cops once when he parked in the lot of a McDonald's with Sophie asleep in the back; he had fallen asleep as well. The officer was very sympathetic and told Tim that one of his own children was hard to soothe, and he understood that Tim was doing whatever he could to keep his daughter asleep.

Merryll and Tim told stories about how Sophie had difficulties with transitions even before Steve was born. They were so focused on Sophie's adjustment to a new baby that Merryll's mother and father came down a month before Merryll's due date to try and keep Sophie entertained. There were more concerns about Sophie than there were about Steve's impending birth. As Sophie's history unfolded, it appeared as if she set the tone for the whole family. Sophie's needs were always taken into consideration no matter what was going on. Tim and Merryll were at their wits' end. They had hoped that having her in regular school when she entered first grade would make a difference. After their first parent-teacher conference, however, they realized things were getting worse and that something may really be going on with Sophie that was causing all the disturbances.

Clinical Issues

In the beginning, when parents make an appointment with me, or when a school asks me to consult, I always listen much more than I talk. It is important for me to know how the parents frame the problem and to get a sense of what "normal" is for them. Sometimes parental expectations are in need of adjustments. There have been times when I needed to let a parent know that their child's behavior is out of the norm for their gender and age. Other times, it's the opposite, and I have the task of telling parents that their child's behavior is in the normal range. Believe it or not, those appointments are more difficult. The parents expect to hear that their child has a specific disorder—like Attention-Deficit/Hyperactivity Disorder (AD/HD)—and that I am going to recommend medication. When the child's symptoms do not meet the criteria for AD/HD, parents seem somewhat bewildered, and we start to talk about the other reasons their child might be having difficulties. Many times those reasons require some kind of adjustment on the part of the parents or specific attention to what parents expect from their child.

The Influence of Personality

It would be unethical to diagnosis a bona fide personality disorder before the age of eighteen. Sophie was only seven, but her parents were already seeing some traits that were similar to the personality traits of Merryll's brother, Austin.

At the time I met Sophie and her family, Austin was in his twenties and was about to graduate college. The family was very worried about him because he tended to bite off more than he could chew. While most graduates talked of earning their first million before they were thirty, Austin talked about retiring rich before he was twenty-five. Austin had always been a sensation seeker. He had been a rebellious adolescent. He would try anything once. He defied authority. He was a free thinker. He also had a high IQ of 140.

Easily bored, Austin tended to think faster than he spoke, which made it difficult for him to listen. It was surprising that Austin never developed a drug problem. His sister attributed that to the fact that their father was an alcoholic, and both Austin and Merryll decided at an early age that they would never take the first drink. Austin knew for sure that he would never stop at one. He possessed a strong enough character that he stuck to his guns and never even took a sip.

Merryll admitted that her mother said that for the past few years, Sophie reminded her a lot of Austin. That was the last thing Merryll and Tim wanted to hear. It certainly wasn't what they expected when they decided to have children. Merryll had lived her life as the sister of a troublemaker; now, she was beginning to believe that she would live the rest of her life as the mother of one.

As I got to know this family over time, it was clear that Sophie was not the child that Merryll and Tim expected. It was all too familiar to Merryll, and she spoke of Sophie as if she were the female version of her brother, Austin. It was up to me to help Merryll and Tim change their expectations of Sophie. By the age of seven, Sophie was already thought of as a problem child who would go out of her way to make people around her miserable.

The one thing that differentiated Sophie and Austin was that Sophie was going to get some professional attention at the early age of seven. Whether or not she had a true clinical issue, the earlier we could intervene, the more likely she would experience success in the future. Austin, on the other hand, was already a grown adult, disinterested in intervention. He didn't see himself as having any problems.

Austin's parents always had reasons for Austin's misbehavior. They thought it was the result of a poor teacher, or, at times, due to allergies. They then thought it was because Austin was taller than the other kids, and that he had social problems because the other kids were jealous of him. They attributed Austin's poor academic progress to boredom. They thought his bad attitude and tantrums were because he didn't sleep well at night. Merryll and Tim weren't going to make that mistake. That was the only thing that helped them stay hopeful. As time progressed, we worked to rule out many of the major reasons why Sophie had been developing differently than her parents expected. Once I helped Merryll and Tim change their expectations of their daughter, things got easier.

David R. Missimo, M.D., a child, adolescent, and adult psychiatrist, says there are two important things that clinicians who treat children should do. "First, they should provide hope. If clinicians do nothing else, they offer patients and their families the view that things can and will improve. An initial interview and a diagnosis should not be viewed as 'an end,' but rather as the beginning of relief from the symptoms that brought them to the office in the first place."

The second goal, according to Dr. Missimo, is for a physician to provide appropriate "expectation management" for treatment. The clinician, patient, and parents all need to be clear about the expectations for treatment, especially when it comes to medication. All too often, parents become disgruntled because medication did not cure the problem. Disappointment eventually leads to termination of the treatment that may have made a significant change in a child's life.

Mood Disorders

According to the American Psychiatric Association, one out of ten people will experience a major mood disturbance. When you just consider children, the incidence is one in thirty-three children. For adolescents, one in eight is currently experiencing significant symptoms of depression. When children experience depression, the symptoms do not present themselves in the same way that they do in adults. The following chart outlines a few of the symptoms seen at different stages of childhood:

Age	Typical Symptoms
0–3	Excessive tantrums Feeding problems A lack of playfulness (too serious or too sad) Blunted affect (lack of emotional expressiveness)
3–5	Tendency to be accident prone Subject to multiple phobias Extreme self-reproach as evidenced by excessive apologies ("Sorry I broke that")
6–8	Vague physical complaints that do not have a physical cause Extreme, aggressive behavior (inappropriate) Clinging behavior (extreme school anxiety)
9–12	Morbid thoughts not related to grief Excessive rumination about schoolwork (academic failure as a particular focus)
13–18	Anger (may manifest itself as sullenness) Hypersensitivity to criticism Uncommunicative tendency Tendency to be covertly hostile

Attention-Deficit/Hyperactivity Disorder

Attention-Deficit/Hyperactivity Disorder (AD/HD) is a disorder that gets a lot of attention. More often than not, the attention is based on the controversy that it is overdiagnosed and that children are overmedicated. Many of the symptoms of AD/HD are the same as those of adjustment difficulties, academic problems, immaturity, poor academic motivation, and/or clinical issues. There is a strong genetic influence. There is a 45–percent chance that one parent has the same disorder.

There is a lot of information available about AD/HD. One of the resources I provide to many of my patients is the organization CHADD (Children and Adults with Attention-Deficit/Hyperactivity Disorder).

The three main symptoms assessed for AD/HD are inattentiveness, impulsivity, or hyperactivity. There is also another subset of symptoms being investigated called Sluggish Cognitive Tempo. While AD/HD is not a learning disability, it does tend to interfere with a child's ability to learn. Many children who are diagnosed with AD/HD are able to get special academic services under the Americans with Disabilities Act. With assistance, many people with AD/HD can learn at a level consistent with their IQ.

The term AD/HD was previously used solely for the hyperactive form of the disorder, while the term ADD (Attention-Deficit Disorder) was reserved for the form without hyperactivity. However, in the past few years, the term ADD has been phased out, leaving the term AD/HD to represent all forms of the disorder. To further describe the disruptive symptoms, AD/HD has three subtypes: Primarily Inattentive, Primarily Impulsive-Hyperactive, and Combined Type, indicating that all three symptoms are present.

It is believed that AD/HD is a disorder of the frontal lobe. The symptoms do not suddenly appear when a child takes precalculus in the ninth grade. The symptoms typically appear before the age of seven and are present in more than one setting. For children, the two settings are at home and at school. Typically, a child with AD/HD may do better in a setting that is more structured, where there are opportunities for redirection, and where he or she can use appropriate compensatory strategies to be successful. Parents may not recognize that giving too many directions at one time is fruitless, especially for young children. In school and at home, children may appear to be easily distracted, unorganized, and unable to independently regulate their ability to remain on task.

Anxiety Disorders

The American Psychiatric Association believes that one out of nine people suffers from some type of anxiety disorder. Test anxiety and social anxiety may be very debilitating for a child. Some parents may misunderstand how troubling a true anxiety disorder can be. Without the proper knowledge, parents may accuse their children of being too worried, too tightly wound, or they may call them a procrastinator, because they spend too much time getting ready to study at the expense of actual study time.

Parents may unknowingly expect their child to do well taking a test in the classroom, if their child was able to do the same work to perfection at home. If a parent has never experienced anxiety to a great degree, it might be difficult to understand how hard it is to "talk yourself out of being afraid."

Behavior Disorders

As I said before, many of the disorders that can be experienced in childhood have overlapping symptoms. Behavioral problems can be due to depression, anxiety, AD/HD, or even learning problems. Remember the class clown in fifth grade? Looking back, his humor may have been a smoke screen for his awareness that academic work was more difficult for him than it seemed to be for his peers.

If a child is given the diagnosis of Oppositional Defiance Disorder or Conduct Disorder, then it is definite that he or she is exhibiting behavior that does not respond to the typical behavior management techniques. Everyone has their moments when they get out of control, but children with true behavior disorders tend to do it persistently and chronically. Many times, the parents themselves need the intervention to know what to do when the inappropriate behavior occurs. To my knowledge, most kids with a behavior disorder do not seek therapy for themselves. It is typically a parent that brings them in because their child's behavior is disruptive to them—not to the child.

It is very frustrating for me, as I'm sure it is for most psychologists, to begin working with a family dealing with a child's behavior problems, only to have those parents drop their child off for therapy. That indicates that it is the child's problem, when in fact the family is the client. If I request the parents attend the appointments and they do not, I explain to them I cannot be effective without their participation.

It does little good to work with a child on their inappropriate behavior if the system surrounding that behavior doesn't change. Working with a child in isolation is very limiting. If a parent has the expectation that therapy will help their defiant child change, then they need to re-evaluate their expectations. For things to change, the parents have to address their role in the problem. The child's behavior may serve a purpose. If I can't help the parents change their expectations and their reactions, then I am limited in my ability to respond to the request for improvement.

Treatment for Clinical Issues

It depends on the presenting symptoms, but most childhood difficulties, if treated early, will see some improvement. At least 80 percent of people treated for depression will see progress. Medication, parent training, and behavior therapy can lessen the disruptive symptoms of AD/HD. Anxiety responds well to a combination of medication and the teaching of coping skills. Behavior problems can improve with family therapy and parent education. More information on these disorders and ways to address them can be found on our website, www.FletcherPhD.com. We also have CDs available on clinical disorders.

As for Sophie, the best thing she had going for her was a supportive family who brought her in at an early age. They were very proactive in their approach, and we saw Sophie benefit. After consulting with the teacher, spending time with the parents to help them adjust their expectations and denial, and monitoring Sophie's symptoms, she improved greatly. We recognized that she had a few social skill deficits, and that her behavior difficulties were fueled by mood instability. She was prescribed mood stabilizers, and by the end of first grade, she was able to blend in with her class. My last contact with Sophie's family revealed that she had had no discipline referrals as a second grader. Her parents come in for appointments periodically to get boosters (or "head checks" as Tim calls it) to make sure they are on target.

For a true clinical disorder to be present, the symptoms have to impair a child's functioning. It would be easy for anyone to diagnose any of the disorders I mentioned just from having their descriptions. If someone thinks they or their child may have a clinical disorder, it is important to get a proper assessment and recommendation for treatment. For children, early intervention can mean a lifetime of success.

Chapter Eight
SMART Moves:

- Your child's temperament is part of his or her unique personality.

- If you think your child's mood or behavior is out of the ordinary, seek help from a clinician; the behavior might be a result of their natural temperament, but it could be a clinical disorder.

- A few well-known clinical disorders that tend to impair a child's functioning are: Attention-Deficit/Hyperactivity Disorder (AD/HD), Anxiety Disorders, Depression, and Conduct Disorder.

- Remember, most childhood difficulties, with early intervention have a greater likelihood of improvement.

Chapter 9

And You Thought You Would Never
Spank Your Children

We commonly see people out and about with their children. To me, the best place to study parents' interactions with their children is in the grocery store. People with children know that you can expect misbehavior when kids are tired, hungry, and bored. The grocery store is fertile ground to see children at their worst and how parents choose to respond; and there are many examples of how parents mistakenly expect that an inappropriate response to their child's misbehavior will shape appropriate behavior.

Do as I Say, Not as I Do

"Don't hit your brother again, or I will spank you." That one is priceless, don't you think? Or what about a child who tends to stretch the truth? Do you really want to lie about their age in order to get a cheaper price on a ski lift ticket? When you expect certain behavior from your kids, you have to ask yourself, "Am I a role model, or am I just expecting them to know better?"

Some examples that are obviously off base in hindsight, yet seem totally right at the moment:

Parenting Goal	Example of Poor Role Modeling
Expect them to tell the truth	Coach your child to lie about his age, so you save money on a ski lift ticket
Expect them to learn how to self-soothe when they get agitated	Freak out when you are driving and get a yellow light when you are running late
Expect them to be adaptable	Be resistant to change when your plans fall through
Expect them to be tolerant of the inability of others and of themselves	Call the grocery store checkout person an idiot for giving back the wrong change

Parenting Goal	Example of Poor Role Modeling
Expect them to keep their rooms clean to create a disciplined environment	Keep trash in your car and leave empty packages on the kitchen counter
Expect them to treat their bodies respectfully	Abuse alcohol and eat lots of fast food
Expect them to use their words to resolve conflict	Spank them when they do wrong
Expect them to be loyal and committed	Have an affair
Expect them to take responsibility for misbehavior	Have an affair, and then lie about it

It really is stating the obvious that your behavior as a parent needs to be congruent with the expectations that you have for your own children. Now, I admit that there are plenty of examples when my response to one of my own children's misbehavior was out of sync. We are all human, after all, and 20 percent of the time, the response isn't too toxic to be inconsistent with our parenting philosophy and our expectations. If most parents would strive to be consistent with their behavior and their words at least 80 percent of the time, however, they might take more pride in the results of their parenting.

Punishment versus Discipline

When developing a parenting philosophy, it is important to ask yourself if you are responding to misbehavior to make yourself feel better, or if you are earnestly trying to create an opportunity for positive change for your child. If you follow the philosophy of punishment, you are setting limitations. If you follow the idea of discipline, you are more likely to see a positive, lasting improvement in future behavior.

Mary Ann and Elliott came in for an appointment when their daughter, Jamie, got in trouble at school for stealing another student's backpack. Mary Ann and Elliott were both police sergeants, and I had met them previously when they came to me for psychological assessments prior to being promoted in the police department. Jamie was one week away from her sixteenth birthday. Besides looking forward to getting her driver's license, she also was looking forward to the party her parents were having for her and all her friends to celebrate her big day. They had planned to have a big bash at a local restaurant with a band. About fifty of her friends were invited and it was going to be the "party of the century."

As if the party wasn't enough, Elliott and Mary Ann had purchased a brand new red convertible, which was sitting in their driveway waiting for Jamie to turn sixteen. They let Jamie drive the car with supervision while she had her learner's permit so she could get some practice driving. I didn't necessarily agree that such festivities—or such a major purchase, for that matter—was appropriate for a sixteen-year-old, but I wasn't asked to comment on that; where I came in was to help them with their daughter's poor judgment in her current circumstances, and to help them figure out the appropriate consequences.

It seems that even before she stole the backpack, Jamie had a history of lying and other small indiscretions. In the past, she had been in trouble for saying she was one place when she was really somewhere else— somewhere she would never have been given permission to go. She had a history of failing to let her parents know about her grades and when she had a test in school. She also, as her mother called it, tried to get away with things, even when they were so small that they really didn't matter. Jamie's parents couldn't understand why Jamie didn't make better decisions. She seemed to lie about so many insignificant things. They were right to be concerned about a sixteen-year-old lying at a higher rate than would be appropriate for her age. They wanted her to be trusted by them, by a boss, by teachers, and even by a future husband. They didn't want her to believe she could get away with being less than truthful.

In the past, Elliott and Mary Ann would typically ground Jamie for poor behavior. That basically led to having to listen to Jamie whine and scream that they were mean and how unfair it was that she couldn't go out with her friends. They also had a history of telling her she was grounded for a period of time and then, out of frustration, fudging on the time and letting her go out anyway. What Jamie learned is that screaming and complaining got her time off her sentence. In other words, if she was annoying enough, they would give in out of frustration.

One of the problems that I saw in our first session together was that Elliott and Mary Ann followed the parenting philosophy of punishment, rather than one based on the concept of discipline. Discipline comes from the word disciple, which means "student/teacher." Using strategies based on the concept of discipline implies that a parent's job is to teach, seeing each infraction as an opportunity. Punishment, on the other hand, imposes power from the outside in order to make someone "pay" for their wrongdoing. Punishment is about power, and discipline is about creating an environment for a child to learn.

Punishment
- is adult oriented.
- requires judgement.
- imposes power from the outside.
- invites more conflict.
- focuses on "restricting" the child.
- concentrates on child "paying" for mistake.
- focuses on external control.
- expresses frustration.
- means the parent works harder than the child.

Discipline
- shows children what they have done wrong.
- gives them ownership of the problem.
- gives them ways to solve the problem.
- leaves their dignity intact.
- uses logical and realistic consequences.
- teaches the benefit of making good decisions.
- teaches a life lesson.
- focuses on developing internal control.
- redirects children toward success.
- role-models good parenting skills.
- child works harder than parent.

Discipline versus Punishment

In the past, Elliott and Mary Ann had used more punishment than discipline. Grounding Jamie made them feel better; and yet, while they were able to exercise their power over their daughter, it only seemed to encourage more conflict. Grounding Jamie didn't give her a chance to practice the appropriate behavior, and it wasn't a natural, logical consequence. In order to use the strategy of discipline, Elliott and Mary Ann were going to have to get in the habit of creating an environment conducive to change, but they weren't sure what that looked like. As a consequence for the backpack incident, they wanted to take away Jamie's party and postpone letting her drive the new car. They also planned to ground her.

Without Jamie present, Elliott and Mary Ann got the tutorial on the difference between punishment and discipline. We first reviewed what canceling the party and forbidding her to get her license would serve. Elliott and Mary Ann both agreed that they were trying to penalize her for her poor judgment. They didn't want her to get away with the backpack incident. However, I was somewhat hesitant about the idea of taking the entire party away. The invitations had gone out and deposits had been given before the backpack incident occurred. I believed that they didn't have to take the whole thing away to accomplish their goal. Besides, I believed that Mary Ann and Elliott had gone somewhat overboard with the rewards of turning sixteen, and that they had already built it up too high to totally strip it away.

As time went on, I drew for them on a dry erase board how their chosen consequences may not fit the crime. It appeared to me that their motivation as parents was to make themselves feel better for not letting Jamie get away with another round of misbehavior.

Making the Consequences Fit the Crime

As we picked apart the points of Jamie's poor judgment and misbehavior, it also appeared as if Elliott and Mary Ann might possibly encourage more misbehavior if they weren't careful.

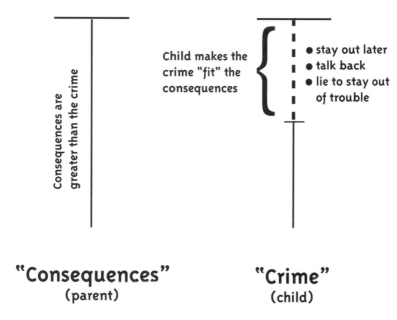

"Consequences"
(parent)

"Crime"
(child)

If Jamie believed that the consequences far outweighed the crime, it was possible that she would do what I see a lot of kids do. In this situation, teenagers not only resist the opportunity to take responsibility for their misbehavior, but they also begin to believe that their future misbehavior is justified. "I'm already in trouble," they reason, "why not sneak out of my room tonight? There's nothing left for them to take away from me." There are no incentives to make good decisions. In the heat of emotion, most human beings are at risk of doing what feels right rather than choosing the right thing to do. We see successful adults make this mistake. Why would we expect self-centered children, when it is age appropriate, to choose to do the right thing rather than the action that simply feels right?

Purposeful Behavior

Instead of taking away everything that Jamie was looking forward to, an adjustment was in order. After helping Elliott and Mary Ann develop a new and improved parenting philosophy independent of their training as police officers, they were able to see the opportunity for Jamie in front of them. When we starting applying the principles of discipline rather than punishment, Mary Ann and Elliott came up with another response—one that they felt more competent to enforce.

Elliott and Mary Ann decided to first start with the consequence for the backpack. A natural and logical consequence would be to expect Jamie to function in school without a backpack. Certainly, that is what the victim of her crime was forced to do when Jamie gained possession of her property. For two weeks, Jamie attempted to function at school with her books, her folders, her makeup, her notes to friends, her gel pens, her hair clips, her personal items, her jacket, and her snack without the safety of a bag to put it in.

You better believe that a young girl turning sixteen prefers the privacy of carrying her things in a well-endowed backpack. It was important that Elliott and Mary Ann present this consequence as nonnegotiable and more as a matter of fact so Jamie could experience the natural, logical consequence of her choices. If they had grounded her instead, they would have had to listen to her bellyaching about how crazy it was that she was being punished for helping out a friend by holding her backpack for her.

Then we took on the party. I pointed out that the invitations had been sent, the deposits had been paid, and the chatter in her peer group had gained momentum. We didn't want to punish her for turning sixteen. Applying the discipline philosophy, we came up with a more appropriate plan. Elliott and Mary Ann decided to have the party, but instead of ending the party at midnight, which was the original plan, the party would end at 10:00 pm. Ending the party earlier than expected and having Jamie see her guests out the door on their way to other events, since their curfews were later than 10:00 pm, would more than likely be a very motivating environment. Hopefully, Jamie would be wondering what could have been while riding home in the car that night earlier than she'd planned. It would give her a taste of something good, but leave her wanting more.

Then there was the car. When it got right down to it, Jamie had been guilty of making poor decisions when left unsupervised. She couldn't be trusted to make the right decision when left to her own resources. In order to discipline her, it was important for Mary Ann and Elliott to give her the opportunity to make things right, with supervision. If they sold the car, then Jamie would not have the chance to show good judgment. Jamie's parents kept the car, and they let Jamie get her driver's license on her sixteenth birthday. However, they decided to restrict Jamie's independent driving rights. Even before the backpack incident, they debated whether or not to allow her to get her license and drive independently. They worried that the license would breed more lies and poor decision making, only this time on wheels. So they dealt with that concern by giving her the chance to earn more independence.

Jamie had an incentive to continue appropriate behavior. She was allowed to drive to school and home and to run very short, specific errands for her parents. After illustrating good judgment, and after her parents followed up and checked it out with other credible sources, Jamie earned the opportunity to drive her car independently for social reasons. What seemed to really make a difference is that Mary Ann and Elliott stuck to their word, and gave Jamie the opportunity to make things right. In the past, they had just hounded her and continually reminded her of all the negatives attached to her misbehavior.

When You Know She Did It

Elliott and Mary Ann had missed an important opportunity by continually trying to make Jamie tell the truth when they knew she was lying. Mary Ann found the backpack in Jamie's closet. She asked Jamie why she had another student's backpack, and Jamie said she was holding it for her. After waiting a couple of days and then asking Jamie again if she was still holding the backpack, Jamie blew her off. Mary Ann's suspicion increased. She finally called the school to see if there was any reason Jamie should be holding the backpack.

Mary Ann knew that Jamie lied a lot of the time to get out of trouble and she wanted to catch her if she wasn't telling the truth. Mary Ann found out from the school counselor that the backpack was reported missing about a week ago. The timing was unfortunate because it was right before exams, and the other student was feverishly working to replace the assignments and schoolwork lost when the backpack disappeared. Mary Ann knew that Jamie was in the wrong.

Mary Ann and Elliott's main method of discipline in the past had been interrogation. They would corner Jamie and keep berating her until she confessed to the crime. Their main goal was to get her to admit that she had done wrong. That didn't surprise me since they were both police officers and they were highly skilled in the techniques of interrogation. Unfortunately, that skill overflowed and influenced their parenting philosophy. They wanted to get her to tell the truth no matter what it took. Needless to say, this caused a lot of frustration for everyone. The end result appeared to be that Jamie got better at lying. If you think about it, she was given lots of opportunities to perfect her technique of stretching the truth.

I tried to help Mary Ann and Elliott see that when they knew Jamie was guilty, they didn't need her to confess to it. When they were sure, they could skip that part. When there was little chance that they were wrong, they were only giving her a chance to exhibit her ability to make excuses, allowing her to resist the opportunity to take responsibility, and teaching her the negative power of negotiation. Next time they believed that Jamie was telling a lie, I told them to move right to the practice of discipline.

True to form, Jamie gave them a chance to practice their new parenting philosophy soon after. She was dishonest about the age of the new guy she seemed interested in. The boy had been over to the house, and Elliott and Mary Ann grew suspicious when he didn't appear to have the traditional schedule one would expect for a typical teenager in high school. Based on the past, Mary Ann and Elliott would be wrong to expect more of Jamie in this type of situation. Not that they shouldn't ever trust her, but with everything that had happened, she needed to prove she could be trusted. Elliott and Mary Ann should expect to have to follow-up with resources more credible than Jamie, at least for a while.

In the past, Elliott and Mary Ann would have cornered Jamie and interrogated her to come clean about his age. This time, with their new skill set in hand, they decided to ask around; they found out that he was actually a freshman at the local junior college. Jamie had met him at a party a few weeks earlier. The next time he came to visit, they asked him how he liked the junior college, right in front of Jamie. Jamie was taken aback, and the young man responded that he enjoyed the classes more than he had in high school. Even though he may have been prompted by

Jamie to lie, he was honest with Elliott and Mary Ann. With that, Elliott and Mary Ann informed the young man and Jamie together that they had concerns about the age difference and preferred that they only spend time together at their house. That was not difficult to enforce.

As a family, Elliott, Mary Ann, and Jamie skipped their regular routine of confrontation and denial and moved right to the expectation of appropriate behavior. Needless to say, Jamie was caught off guard but content to continue seeing him at home. Alone, Jamie later confessed to me that she felt she had been given a chance to be trusted. She even commented that she thought she knew for sure that her parents would forbid her from seeing him, so she expected the relationship to end. She was now just thankful that she could still see him.

Our hope was that this new suitor would grow tired of having to be supervised and move on to another person who was at the same stage of life and had the same independence. Well, that natural, logical consequence occurred in less than a month. It also occurred to us, and maybe you, that Jamie had lied to this young man about her age. Maybe this was an event that could be seen as a learning opportunity for Jamie. We hoped that she was now experiencing opportunities to reshape her own behavior rather than opportunities to try and get away with something.

SMART Moves:

- A parent must behave the way they want the child to behave. Be consistent with your own behavior and your expectations.

- Learn the difference between discipline and punishment. Discipline is when a parent uses infractions as opportunities to teach a lesson. Punishment tends to use power to force someone to do something.

- Make sure the consequences fit the crime.

- It is fruitless to badger your child into telling the truth when you already know he or she is guilty of an infraction. Instead, skip the interrogation and move directly to discipline.

Chapter 10

Raising a Happy Child

It is so difficult to stand back when you know your child is not happy. I don't care what the problem is. It could be that their best friend invited someone else for a sleepover, or that they didn't remember to bring their bike in before it rained, or his brother took his CD and now it is nowhere to be found. Some children are more resilient about bouncing back from discontent. Sometimes it is temperament that allows them to recover so easily. For most of us, it is a learned skill that needs to be purposeful, since it doesn't come naturally. You probably have heard that children are more resilient than adults. If this is true, when do they lose that ability, and what can we do as parents to contribute to their overall well-being and happiness?

Who Is Responsible for Your Child's Happiness?

Jennifer was a junior in high school when I first met her. She appeared to have been very successful with her peers, and for the most part, she was happy and content with her life. Things seemed to come easily for her. She had a boyfriend when other girls did not, she made cheerleading every year she tried out, and she did well in school even without studying. She began therapy when her parents divorced. Her mother believed that Jennifer was not used to change and that she had sheltered her daughter in the past from disappointment and loss. Jennifer's mother presented the problem in such a way that it appeared as if she had been responsible and attempted to control her daughter's happiness. Jennifer had never really needed good coping mechanisms, and her mother was concerned that the divorce would be her first big upset. This time, Jennifer's mother was having trouble controlling the situation and was trying to protect Jennifer from discontent.

At the first appointment, I thoroughly enjoyed Jennifer's company. She was a good storyteller and very good at conversation. Yet, while she told me a lot about herself, she hardly used any "feeling" words. When asked directly, she gave general responses. After the first two sessions, I could see that Jennifer's demeanor was taking a turn. She became somewhat withdrawn in the sessions because it was very uncomfortable for her to discuss her concerns about her parents' divorce and what the change would mean to her and her family. What was also clear was that her mother did most of the talking for her. The feeling words came more from her mother than from Jennifer's first-person account. Even then, the feeling words, expressed by her mother and assigned to Jennifer, were interpretations of Jennifer's behavior, rather than her own words. It was clear very early on that Jennifer was having a hard time coping with the divorce. It was also very clear that her mother was resistant to letting Jennifer have the opportunity to struggle. I knew that I needed to spend session time with Jennifer independent of her mother in order to provide an opportunity for Jennifer to progress emotionally.

I knew Jennifer's happiness was dependent on her being able to form her own opinions and thoughts about the state of her life. Even while I encouraged her mother to allow Jennifer to live in an environment where she felt anxious and on edge, it was very difficult for her mother, outside of sessions, to disengage even slightly from Jennifer's needs. Because Jennifer did not show signs of clinical depression or a bona fide anxiety disorder, I felt it was important for her emotional development to use words to describe how she felt and develop the internal ability to believe that she was in control of personal successes and failures. I didn't want Jennifer to think that the events controlled her. Not only was this an attempt to gain effective life skills, but it was also an effort to foster the opportunity for her own satisfaction and happiness.

Happiness Is Best Not Left to Chance

In his book *The Childhood Roots of Adult Happiness*, Edward Hallowell, M.D., states that happiness is best not left to chance. He outlines what he believes children need, beyond the physical necessities, in order to thrive and be happy.

1. CONNECTION: By growing up with a strong feeling of connectedness, a child develops a sense of basic trust early on. According to Dr. Hallowell, a child with connectedness also develops feelings of security and safety, which, in turn, instill courage and the desire to take risks in the world. These risks could occur as early as six months or beyond sixty years old.

2. PLAY: A child at play is a child at work. Play builds imagination, teaches problem-solving skills and cooperation. Further, sustained play gives opportunities for dreams and beliefs. Play also generates joy and allows a child to enter that state of mind Mihaly Csikszentmihalyi, Ph.D. (pronounced "ME-high CHICK-sent-me-high-ee") calls "flow." Flow is a state of deep focus that occurs when people engage in challenging tasks that demand intense concentration and commitment. Dr. Csikszentmihalyi, a professor of education and psychology at the University of Chicago, has studied the lives of thousands of people for more than thirty years in search of what makes people's lives meaningful and satisfying. He believes that flow is when we are at our most fulfilled and it is usually at times when we are using our skills to the maximum and at the same time being challenged. According to Dr. Csikszentmihalyi, a joyful life "is an individual creation that cannot be copied from a recipe . . . Happiness, in fact, is a condition that must be prepared for, cultivated, and defended privately by each person." According to Csikszentmihalyi, humans are at their happiest in flow, forgetting where they are or even who they are.

3. PRACTICE: A child who plays will eventually learn the power of practice and the first step of mastery and success—failure. With practice comes discipline, as well as the ability to learn how to receive help, teaching, or coaching.

4. MASTERY: According to Dr. Hallowell, the roots of self-esteem lie not in praise, but in mastery. He believes that parents shouldn't go out of their way to praise their children, but instead go out of their way to make sure children experience mastery in many different ways. With mastery comes confidence, leadership skills, initiative, and an enduring desire to work hard.

5. RECOGNITION: After mastery is achieved, recognition and approval by a larger group comes naturally. Dr. Hallowell states that it is important not only that others value and recognize the child, but also that the child feels valued and recognized for who he or she actually is.

Each of these five steps logically leads to the next, even though the progression is not always smooth. According to Dr. Hallowell, the basic strategy of following these steps usually leads to many benefits. One of the mistakes parents may make is trying to force and externally apply these ideas, instead of considering how their child can grow these abilities naturally within him or herself.

This was the case for Jennifer's mother. In therapy, it was important for me to help both Jennifer and her mother learn the importance of giving Jennifer the opportunity to develop her own capability for growth. As Dr. Hallowell discovered, when each of the traits or capabilities grows from within the child, they tend to endure and grow for the rest of the person's life.

Dr. Hallowell's five concepts for happiness are further evidence of why the Low-Value SMART Model discussed in Chapter 5 is so important. A child who is given many low-value opportunities has the blessing of practice and failure in their interaction with a parent. The opportunity provided by low-value items is the opportunity of mastery at a low level, the development of confidence and initiative, not to mention the desire and development of a successful work ethic. Ultimately, the opportunity to feel connected, play, practice, attempt and achieve mastery, and feel valued by recognition not only fuels the state of happiness, but also contributes to the development of healthy self-esteem.

Our Reputation Fuels Our Self-Esteem

Self-esteem is this: self-esteem is the reputation we have with ourselves. It doesn't matter how others perceive us; it is the perception we have of ourselves internally that determines the value we place on ourselves. Our self-esteem affects our attitudes, feelings, self-worth, and knowledge that we have about our skills, abilities, appearance, and social acceptability. Jennifer's self-esteem appeared to be high to most observers. As I got to know her more, I could see that her self-esteem was somewhat lacking. Her identity was tied up in the perceptions of others who saw her as a cheerleader with a boyfriend and a happy life. With her parents' divorce, it became more difficult for her to hide the perception she had of herself. As she became more talkative in therapy without her mother present, she made comments like, "I have to have a boyfriend, so I can continue to hang out with the same group of people." She also disclosed that, even as a senior, she was anxious about cheerleading tryouts and feared that she might not be chosen. "I don't know what I will do if I don't make it." As I probed further, her perception of herself became exposed. It was exposed not only to me, but also to Jennifer herself. It appeared as if Jennifer did not have the confidence or feelings of competence that we thought she had.

One of my main objectives with Jennifer was to help her see her self-efficacy beliefs in ordinary routine behaviors. I discovered that Jennifer had trouble making decisions, even from a menu at a restaurant. She disclosed that she typically ordered what someone else ordered, not trusting her own ability to choose. She also disclosed that she didn't really care too much for her current boyfriend, but felt pressure to stay with him since it was what was expected. As time went on, Jennifer became more dissatisfied with her now "clear picture" and learned that she could improve her image of herself and begin to live her life with more confidence and determination. I knew she was improving when she rearranged some of the furniture in my waiting room before one of her appointments. While she didn't apologize for the boldness, she did let me know right off that she would change it back if I wanted her to. Funny thing was, she made good choices, and the waiting room looked so much better. I was glad to have the opportunity to witness her mastery. I saw a renewed confidence, initiative, and an enduring desire to continue to be in charge of her own feelings. Even in the face of her parents' divorce, Jennifer was able to maintain a sense of contentment, although it took a while for her to make those traits automatic.

There are a number of ways we can provide an atmosphere of competence, just like those experienced by Jennifer. One of the people I admire most, Tony Jeary, suggests that giving children the opportunity to learn effective presentation skills improves self-esteem. In his book Life is a Series of Presentations: *8 Ways to Punch Up Your People Skills at Work, at Home, Anytime, Anywhere*, he makes the point that life is a series of presentations. By providing opportunities for children and adolescents to develop effective skills in the classroom, on the job, at home, and in everyday living, we are giving them the opportunity to develop a rich source of self-efficacy and confidence.

Self-Efficacy and Confidence

According to Stanford Psychologist Albert Bandura, self-efficacy is the expectation that people hold about their abilities to accomplish certain tasks. Self-efficacy comes from mastery experience, vicarious experience, verbal persuasion, and physiological states. Self-efficacy differs from self-esteem in the following ways:

Self-Efficacy Beliefs	Self-Esteem Beliefs
Judgment based on confidence	Judgment based on self-worth
Assessment of competence	Cognitive appraisal
Sensitive to the context	Not sensitive to the context
Can be task-specific	Not task-specific
Made and used in reference to some type of goal	Cognitive self-evaluation of self-worth independent of goal
Domain-specific	Can be domain-specific
A question of can: "Can I do this?"	A question of being/feeling: "Who am I?" "How do I feel?"

Whether or not someone will undertake a particular activity, attempt a particular task, or strive to meet a particular goal depends on whether or not he or she believes they will be effective performing those actions. If your son believes that asking the homecoming queen out for a date and that her accepting is attainable and within his control, he will ask her out even though he knows others have been turned down by her in the past. He is confident that he can do it, and it is related to some type of goal. The belief that he can ask her out greatly aids his well-being and, ultimately, his happiness.

Locus of Control

Locus of control refers to the extent to which an individual believes his or her behavior determines specific life events. Psychologist Julian Rotter developed the theory in the 1960s to describe the generalized expectancies regarding the forces that determine rewards and punishments. The way individuals interpret events has a profound effect on their psychological well-being and happiness. Having a positive outlook, feeling in control of one's destiny, and having a general sense of well-being is a force that influences risk-taking, choices, and the general course of one's life. Locus of control is believed to form during childhood and stabilize during adolescence. A person's expectations and locus of control tend to develop more quickly and are most malleable when the individual has relatively few life experiences.

Children who have an external locus of control tend to believe that it is solely the teacher's responsibility to teach them the course material. The student believes it is not their responsibility to learn the material. Students who believe they can't do a task—or can't do it well—might not even start the assignment. These are often the students with low self-esteem, since one's sense of self-worth grows through achievement, and achievement comes through effort. Most people fall somewhere in the middle of internal and external locus of control, believing that it is a combination of their own efforts and outside circumstances that affect the outcome of events in their lives.

A SMART Look at Locus of Control

INTERNALS

Tend to believe they are in control of personal successes and failures and are able to cause certain events; attribute successes and failures to own abilities and efforts

EXTERNALS

Tend to believe success or failure is beyond their control and are a result of luck, chance, fate, or other powerful things; attribute successes and failures to external sources

Internals	Externals
Exhibit high work motivation, high achievement, and expect to perform well	Exhibit lower work motivation; work better when pace is automated
Express more contentment with life	Feel more anger and perceive others to be less friendly
See the world in a more adaptive perspective	See the world in a less adaptive perspective
More intelligent and more success-oriented; more independent, achieving, and dominant	Perceived to be less intelligent and less success-oriented
Relatively successful in the delay of gratification	Likely to make less of an effort to exert self-control in the present because they doubt their ability to influence events in the future
Do better in jobs where they can set their own pace; more effort leads to higher performance	Tends to be negative, give up easily, and not try too hard; need tighter supervision
Inclined to take responsibility for their actions, are not easily influenced by the opinions of others, and tend to do better at tasks when they can work at their own pace	Tend to blame outside circumstances for their mistakes and credit their successes to luck rather than to their own efforts; readily influenced by the opinions of others
Know that knowledge helps establish internal control	More concerned about what other people think than becoming competent
Pay more attention to the content of the opinion regardless of who holds it	More likely to pay attention to the status of the opinion holder

Internals	Externals
More health conscious and seek medical attention when needed	Will not initiate contact or attempt to repair damaged relationship
Less likely to suffer from depression and other ailments because they believe their actions can improve their current position; less prone to stress-related illnesses	More likely to suffer from depression and other ailments because they believe their actions cannot improve their current position; feel victimized by illness and stress and tend to take less preventative action
Tend to exhibit less anxiety	Tend to exhibit more anxiety; correlated with emotional instability
Show typical shifts in expectations of success following success or failure; those who succeed have increased expectancies following success and decreased expectancies following failure	Show more atypical expectancy shifts, exhibiting decreased expectancies of success following success, and increased expectations of success following failure
Can be very hard on themselves, taking responsibility for failures that they can't control	Can believe that their work or talents will have little effect on how things turn out
May have higher self-worth due to the fact that they are more likely to reach mastery and put forth more effort	May have lower self-worth since one's sense of self-worth grows through achievement, and achievement comes through effort

In *You Can Choose to be Happy*, Tom Stevens, Ph.D., outlines barriers that tend to increase external control and decrease internal control.

The following barriers are exactly the opposite of what you want in order for your child to be happy:

- Believing that you must have the approval and acceptance of others to be happy
- Making acceptance from your family and peers more important than your own happiness
- Believing that your individual happiness is selfish or unimportant
- Having low self-worth, low confidence, or low competence in some task
- Having a fear of being alone and a fear of not being able to make yourself happy
- Choosing to be too dependent on someone
- Allowing your opinion of yourself to be based on the opinions of others
- Fearing some awful truth about yourself
- Being terrified of disapproval or rejection
- Letting obedience or rebellion become too important
- Letting media ideas become too powerful
- Allowing obedience, passivity, and non-assertiveness to become too strong

One of the ways I keep my locus of control at a healthy balance is by participating in an exercise boot camp at 5:30 in the morning. As a psychologist, author, speaker, and mother, I rely on my creativity in many ways; boot camp has shifted me into a higher gear—not only physically, but also mentally. As I participate in Lone Star Basic Training almost every weekday morning, I start my day believing that I am in control of personal successes and failures and that I am able to cause certain events. I start my day attributing my successes and failures to my own abilities and efforts. The leader and founder, Nolan Broughton, plays the role of drill sergeant, never missing any opportunity to remind us that we set our own limitations. I have always had high work motivation. By exposing myself to this physical and mental challenge, I am reminded everyday of my abilities, both physically and mentally. Everyone needs a Nolan in their life to remind them what they are made of.

While I was pregnant with our last son, Sam, in 2000, I was on bed rest for early contractions and had to deal with managing my practice, moving my office space, and managing the challenge of gestational diabetes. My mother-in-law, Amy, came from Florida to help for over three months. Even though Sam was born healthy and ready to take on the world, my physical well-being suffered while I was pregnant from having him take what he needed to grow, leaving my body stressed out and undernourished. I only gained nine pounds during that pregnancy and gave birth to an eight-pound baby. At thirty-seven years old, I walked out of the hospital in clothes that weren't maternity and as if I smelled fresh air for the first time. I don't ever want to feel that sick again. The experience taught me to value life and to value my health. It also pushed me further toward a healthier locus of control.

We don't have to send our kids to 5:30 a.m. boot camp or wait for them to experience a potential tragedy to lay the groundwork for happiness and a healthy locus of control. There are a number of things that a parent can teach children that can improve a child's locus of control, which will ultimately provide a promising opportunity for happiness and appropriate independence from you:

- Encourage your child to be self-reflective.
- Help your child believe he or she can influence what happens to him or her.
- Connect small, targeted accomplishments to your child's goals.
- Help your child keep a journal of thoughts, moods, and activities.
- Eliminate modes of thinking that keep your child stuck.
- Use reasoning, articulate limits, and reflect on behavior with your child.
- Help your child consciously choose to direct thoughts and energy toward accomplishments.
- Help your child choose to be undaunted by anxieties or feelings of inadequacy.
- Follow the Low-Value SMART Model with your children.

Even though Jennifer appeared to be successful based on her previous accomplishments, her locus of control needed to be tweaked. During the time I worked with her, one of the major events besides her parents' divorce was trying out for cheerleading as a senior. Jennifer tended to believe that her success or failure was beyond her control and that making cheerleading would be the result of luck, chance, fate, or other powerful forces. Jennifer denied herself the ability to see her control over the situation.

As the tryouts got closer, she became more convinced that her hard work and talent would have an effect on how things might eventually turn out. This life event gave us the opportunity to exercise her transition to an internal locus of control. With a lot of prompting and reinforcement, over time, Jennifer transitioned to being able to recognize that her best efforts were enough. She also was able to attribute her expected success to hard work. More important, Jennifer was able to prepare herself for the fact that not making cheerleading would not be the end of the world, as she had so many other attributes that could be applied elsewhere. By the time tryouts were held, Jennifer was using feeling words when she talked about her thoughts and opinions on her life, including the effects of her parents' divorce.

Emotional Intelligence

Another component to a child's happiness has to do with emotional intelligence. As was the case with Jennifer, most children have to learn to recognize their own feelings and those of other people. Emotional intelligence is the capacity for recognizing our own feelings and those of others, for motivating ourselves, and for managing emotions in ourselves and in our relationships. Research has shown us that a person's emotional intelligence is a better predictor of future success than traditional methods like GPA, IQ, and standardized test scores.

Emotional intelligence has four characteristics and abilities:
1. SELF-AWARENESS: knowing your emotions, recognizing feelings as they occur, and discriminating between them.
2. MOOD MANAGEMENT: handling feelings so they're relevant to the current situation and you react appropriately.
3. EMPATHY: recognizing feelings in others and tuning into their verbal and nonverbal cues.
4. MANAGING RELATIONSHIPS: handling interpersonal interaction, conflict resolution, and negotiations.

As you can imagine, building a child's emotional intelligence has a life-long impact. It describes abilities distinct from, but complementary to, academic intelligence or the purely cognitive capacities measured by IQ. IQ is relatively stable throughout a person's life. On the other hand, much of emotional skill is learned and can be taught to young children. According to Daniel Goleman, Ph.D., "Having great intellectual abilities may make you a superb fiscal analyst or legal scholar, but a highly developed emotional intelligence will make you a candidate for CEO or a brilliant trial lawyer."

In his book *Raising an Emotionally Intelligent Child*, John Gottman, Ph.D., describes the need for parents to be Emotion Coaches. He believes emotion coaching teaches children to trust their feelings, regulate their own emotions, and solve problems. Children like Jennifer, who are given the opportunity to raise their emotional intelligence, typically go on to have high self-esteem, learn well, and get along well with others.

Dr. Gottman offers this description of an Emotion Coach:
1. Values the child's negative emotions as an opportunity for intimacy
2. Can tolerate spending time with a sad, angry, or fearful child; does not become impatient with these emotions
3. Is aware of and values his or her own emotions
4. Sees the world of negative emotions as an important arena for parenting
5. Is sensitive to the child's emotional states, even when they are subtle
6. Is not confused or anxious about the child's emotional—expression; knows what needs to be done
7. Respects the child's emotions
8. Does not poke fun at or make light of the child's negative feelings
9. Does not say how the child should feel
10. Does not feel he or she has to fix every problem for the child
11. Uses emotional moments as a time to:
    • Listen to the child
    • Empathize with soothing words and affection
    • Help the child label the emotion he or she is feeling
    • Offer guidance on regulating emotions
    • Set limits and teach acceptable expression of emotions
    • Teach problem-solving skills

In order to stay in the SMART Zone, it is important to look at the qualities that will keep our children in their own SMART Zone. Dr. Goleman writes in his 1998 book, *Working with Emotional Intelligence*, "We are being judged by a new yardstick: not just how smart we are, or by our training and expertise, but also by how well we handle ourselves and each other."

By focusing on the many aspects of emotional development and the coping skills that lead to happiness, we not only provide our children with contentment now, but also give them the skills they will need for their own families in the future.

Chapter Ten
SMART Moves:

- The five steps to happiness in children are connection, play, practice, mastery, and recognition.

- Create an atmosphere of competence by providing children with opportunities to develop effective skills. This will lead to increased self-efficacy and confidence.

- Try to keep your children's locus of control at a healthy balance between internal and external.

- Building a child's emotional intelligence has a permanent impact.

- The four characteristics of emotional intelligence are self-awareness, mood management, empathy, and managing relationships.

✳ Chapter 11

*Making Your Kids Get
Along with Each Other*

It is kind of a cruel twist of nature. You have one child and that child throws you for a loop. Then you figure out what you are doing as a parent and begin finding your rhythm and start to feel comfortable about this new role. Then you feel confident and have another baby. From the start, you can see that even the pregnancy is different. When the second child is born, you are caught off guard by the many differences in your children.

Of course, the other factor related to having more than one child is wanting them to get along with each other. There will be sibling rivalry, conflict resolution, communication, and sibling relationships, all of which teach children valuable social skills for the future.

SMART Sibling Rivalry

My friend Camille Joiner has a unique situation when it comes to sibling rivalry and conflict resolution. With four boys under the age of seven, Camille's experience with her children can sometimes be a challenge:

Jeff and I had our son Kendall in the very hot summer of 1996. We thought we should be busier, so we decided to have twin boys, Kerry and Hunter, in the very hot summer of 1998. As if our plate was not already full enough, we were blessed with our fourth boy, Trevor, in the winter of 1999. Four boys who are four and under can prove to be difficult in many areas: feeding, playing, bathing, outings, money, etc. When you have so many boys so close in age, sibling rivalry can be a real challenge because they argue about everything. We are required to measure everything out in the same size portions, give the same quantity and type of toys, the same color clothes, and on and on. Funny, I have never had to count out peas. As you can imagine, we do not have four of everything, so, a kitchen timer works great. Our house looks like a toy store, so you would think that between the ten thousand toys (no exaggeration, I counted), there would be enough to go around. Some of the neighbors think a primary-colored bomb went off in the yard and others just think we run a day care.

Sometimes sibling rivalry is really about a child trying to belong and feel significant. Many people believe that sibling rivalry is just about jealousy. Many times sibling rivalry is really about a child trying to belong and feel significant inside and outside the family. When this phenonmenon occurs within the family, there can be a competition of sorts. Parents understandably tend to get concerned when rivalry occurs because they are unsure of how to determine if the rivalry is too severe. There are six ways that can help determine if your child is being harmed by sibling rivalry. First, get attentive to determine if the complaint about fairness is legitimate. Second, unprovoked aggression can be about frustrations in school. Look to determine if one of your children is being targeted by the other for no reason. Third, you are right to be concerned if one of your children begins to avoid activities that involve competition. Fourth, look for a sudden lack of interest in activities he or she previously enjoyed. Fifth, be attentive to negative self-statements that your child may make that indicate feelings of low self-worth or extreme inability. Finally, monitor if your child shows symptoms of depression or extreme sadness. It is possible that a child can experience symptoms of depression in response to severe and/or long-term rivalry.

Most sibling rivalry can be healthy in that it can provide the opportunity for children to learn important life skills. The degree of rivalry and whether or not it has harmful consequences depends a lot on what the parents do about it. Seeing rivalry as an opportunity to develop unique strengths, positive self-statements, and conflict management skills can turn sibling clashes into valuable life skill opportunities.

SMART Conflict Resolution

For the Joiner boys, conflict resolution can be quite a challenge. According to Camille:

> When all four of our boys are in the backyard, our neighbors can all hear the fighting over the slide, a swing (they all want the blue one), the water hose, and the battery-powered car. We have many toys that just disappear for a time since they are a major source of arguing. Have you ever tried reasoning with a two-year-old? Try explaining why the twins get lots of presents

and a party on their birthday, and he doesn't have anything to open. Reminding him that he had lots of cool gifts on his birthday just doesn't work. As they get older and hopefully more understanding (hopefully, they are out of time out), maybe they will know why they must wait to get their driver's license until they are twenty-five!

If you perceive one of your children to be more of an "underdog," it is important not to try and protect that child from other "alpha dogs." The best thing to do is try and stay out of it. Aligning yourself with the underdog only reinforces that he or she is weak and needs your protection. Often, when a parent tries to help fix and even out a situation, it only complicates the issue. When a parent chooses sides, he or she is training potential victims and bullies.

Fairness is a big theme for many families. The more a parent tries to be fair, the more likely children will make an issue out of fairness. It is important for parents to remember that what is fair to one person may seem unfair to another. It is normal for children to compare themselves with their siblings or feel jealous. Parents should take note, however; it is not their job to fix everything or try to control the family so a child never experiences these feelings. SMART parents can resist the urge to be manipulated by the phrase "it's not fair," by responding with either curiosity or turning the problem back to their children. Responses like "I don't do fair," or "I will hold on to all of the CDs until both of you come up with a good proposal for what would be fair," may diffuse the problem quicker than reasoning or explaining. Have faith in your children to try and work out many of the conflicts that you think only a parent can handle.

Even though what works for the young Joiner boys might not work for children who are preteens and teenagers, the following ideas on how to diffuse sibling conflict can be considered and adapted for any age:

- Create and introduce diversions
- Prepare the physical environment for when rivalry might occur
- Redirect to another activity or item
- Separate children so that they play apart from one another before they get out of control (not necessarily to punish them)
- Choose activities that maximize fun while minimizing rivalry

- Rotate toys to maintain interest
- Leave the room (sometimes kids fight to get you involved)
- Never compare children against each other, as it creates competition
- Create an atmosphere of cooperation and collaboration

Using the SMART Sandwich to Communicate

It is difficult, at times, for children to communicate their needs, especially when it comes to siblings. Their attempts at communication in the family lay the groundwork for learning to communicate effectively with peers, especially in conflict situations. Some children can be taught facilitative feedback, where they parrot back what someone has just said to them for understanding. Adults typically don't use that technique, so a child would be expected to have similar difficulty.

Over the years, while teaching children the skills of conflict management and communication, I came up with a structure for communication they can remember and follow. More important, they can remember it when it counts. They are able to use it when they are having trouble getting along with siblings as well as peers. Children can also use it when they are communicating about something they have passion for with their parents. I call it the SMART Sandwich Model.

SMART Sandwich Model

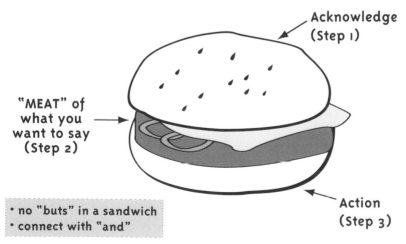

Acknowledge
(Step 1)

"MEAT" of
what you
want to say
(Step 2)

Action
(Step 3)

- no "buts" in a sandwich
- connect with "and"

There are three steps in the SMART Sandwich Model for a child to remember and use. The first step is to communicate some acknowledgement. People tend to repeat themselves when they don't feel that they have been heard. Again, people tend to repeat themselves when they don't feel that they have been heard. If a child can be taught to acknowledge or validate the expected response first, it will go a long way in helping with conflict, especially with siblings.

The second step is actually the meat of what you want to say. I believe that children should be allowed to say what they want to say. As I described in more detail in Chapter 10, being able to communicate, whether it is with preferences or feelings, contributes to appropriate locus of control and a well-developed emotional intelligence. Of course, this model would also incorporate the opportunity for a person to communicate the "meat" of what he or she wants to say, or the main topic.

The third and final step creates the opportunity to manage conflict. It is the action part of the model. As most adults can attest, conflict is difficult to manage in any relationship, if there is not an action step involved. Alas, this is what most people tend to leave out, creating an environment where the communication becomes circular and redundant. It is difficult to accomplish much of anything if the suggestion of action is not made.

Here is an example of how the SMART Sandwich Model can be applied between two sisters—Sophie (age ten) and Katie (age twelve):

Katie: Sophie, did you take my blue sweater again?

Sophie: I know you would rather I not take your sweater without asking (Step 1).

I needed it for the sleepover and you weren't home to ask permission (Step 2).

Next time, what if I left you a note and made you a coupon to borrow any of my clothes in return for letting me borrow something or yours (Step 3)?

Now, Katie may not agree, and Sophie will just have to live with it or come up with another suggestion if the same scenario happens again. Nonetheless, hopefully the focus would be on the action rather than the "meat." As a child is learning this model, it is important for a parent to positively reinforce the model over and over again, so it becomes second nature. A parent would also need to role model the structure of the process, so it becomes the automatic way of interacting.

Without using the SMART Sandwich Model, an interaction between a child and his mother might sound like this:

Son: I want to spend the night at Cody's house Friday night.

Mom: I'd rather you not. Your father is out of town, and I'd prefer for you to sleep at home that night.

Son: I don't know why. It will just be boring over here, and you never let me do anything. What difference does it make that dad is out of town? That's not fair.

Using the SMART Sandwich Model, the conversation could go like this:

Son: I know you prefer that I not spend the night out when dad is out of town (Step One).

I'd really like to spend the night with Cody since we don't get to see each other very much at school anymore (Step Two).

If you'd rather I not spend the night tonight, maybe we can look at the calendar and see the next time we could schedule it (Step Three).

I know, as a Mom, I'm more likely to say yes to a request like that. Consider the valuable skill you are teaching your child by communicating with the SMART Sandwich Model. It is a skill they can use now and in the future.

SMART Skills for the Future

The theme of many sibling rivalry issues is often one of fairness, which creates an opportunity to learn SMART skills for the future. Through the experience of sibling rivalry, children can discover that "equal" doesn't necessarily mean "the same." They can also learn that it is more important to pay attention to the situation than to one person's idea of what is fair. By recognizing the opportunities sibling rivalry and conflict can provide, children can learn a variety of ways to make choices and decisions when there are differences of opinions.

It is important for every family to recognize that sibling rivalry and conflict are the precursors to career skills. One of the main reasons that people tend to lose their jobs when a company needs to cut employees isn't always because the person can't do the job. Many times the decision is made because the person can't get along. For families that only have one child, there are still opportunities to simulate sibling relationships with neighbors, cousins, or classmates. Whether a family has one child or four, like the Joiners, it is important to get together with other families and encourage SMART bonding.

For the past three years, our family and the Joiner family have traveled for a week's stay in Angel Fire, New Mexico to take our seven boys snow skiing. Last year, we had seven boys between the ages of three and eight in one cabin!

People think we are crazy to caravan in our cars with a bunch of boys, but we consider ourselves SMART—SMART enough to create another opportunity to teach our children to be in their SMART Zone.

Chapter Eleven
SMART Moves:

- Sibling rivalry can give children the opportunity to learn conflict resolution and teach them to make choices and decisions when there are differences of opinions.

- Learn the three steps of the SMART Sandwich Model for communication: convey acknowledgment, allow children to say what they want to say (the "meat"), and take action to manage the conflict.

- Recognize that sibling rivalry and conflict are the precursors to career skills.

Chapter 12

Tryng to Put Your
Family First

While the previous chapters focused on what is best for children and how you as a parent can stay in your SMART Zone, this chapter is solely for you, the parent.

You may recall this example from a previous chapter: If a flight attendant approaches you on a plane while you are traveling with small children, the attendant will explain what to do if cabin pressure is lost during the flight. A small bag for oxygen will fall down from the overhead compartment. As a parent, our first instinct would be to put the oxygen mask on our children. Of course, we would feel an obligation and duty to provide for them. But the flight attendant example is a good one. Just as it would be in your child's best interest for you to put the mask on yourself first, get stabilized, and then put another mask on your child, in life it is also important to take care of yourself so you are in the best condition to take care of your children.

Many parents struggle with this concept. In order to put your family first, you have to make sure your needs are met so that you are better able to meet theirs.

Using Your Time Effectively

As I sit here finishing this chapter on a beautiful Sunday, my three children, my husband, and some of our friends are out on the boat at a local Texas lake enjoying the day. I don't miss too many days on the lake. Today's outing comes at a critical time in the writing of this book, though. I hand it to the editor on Friday and the process of production begins. In order to be SMART, I chose to stay back today to use the time effectively. If I went to the lake, the weight of needing to finish the task would haunt me. I would be somewhat preoccupied by the need to use the evening hours to get everything done.

As a business owner, a supervisor, a professional speaker, an author, not to mention the mother of three small children, I am able to succeed at all I need to do only because I make difficult choices. I benefit, as does my family, if I use my time effectively and use the uninterrupted hours I have on days like today to complete what I have to do. While it is a difficult choice, it is a good investment. I am investing not only in my business, but also in my family. By using the time I have today, I will be more accessible to them as the week continues, both with my attention and my energy.

Competition for Your Attention and Energy

While much of the information about helping parents to balance work and family life talks about time management, I am going to go in a different direction. I believe that you can get all the electronic organizers you desire, hire someone to do the lawn and clean your house, say no to proposed commitments, and still have difficulty balancing day-to-day life. The reason is because balancing is actually about your mind-set, not your actions. If you don't do a number of things to keep yourself in the SMART Zone, you are going to struggle with the competing demands of having a family and living your life, whether you are working outside the home or not.

Recently I traveled to three cities in one week for speaking engagements. I typically travel to one city at a time because I don't want to be away from my family too long. For this particular trip, I had a slew of details to manage, and I had to make sure that I would be fresh when the opportunity came to speak to three different groups of businessmen and women. Thank God I have an efficient and totally effective assistant, Sharon Beck, who anticipates my needs and looks for ways to save my time for professional commitments. At the first stop of my mini tour, I was in a beautiful hotel in St. Louis. When I arrived that evening, I unpacked my suits for the week. One of the suits was badly wrinkled (thanks to the airport security rummaging through my suitcase). Even though security left a note, I was still somewhat miffed, since I wouldn't have time to have the suit dry-cleaned. I would be flying out the next evening to Columbus. I knew I would be risking the possibility of my suitcase being searched again on the way to Columbus. In order to do the smart thing and attend to the suit the best I could, I hung it on the back of the bathroom door while I took a shower. Right before I went to bed, I lay down and had the thought, "What if I forget that part of my suit when I am in a hurry to pack in the morning for my evening flight?"

In order to stay in my SMART Zone, I got up out of bed and moved the suit to the closet where the rest of my clothes for the week were hung.

I went to bed with that concern off my list. Just like a physical list of things to do, your mental list hovers in your head, weighing on you to remember to do something really important.

In order to put your family first, it is necessary to manage the competition for your attention and energy. By staying behind today to finish my homework (as my kids call it) and last month moving that suit to a more conspicuous place in my hotel room, I am able to free up my attention and energy for other, more important things. It is more than time management; it is SMART life management.

SMART Life Chart

One of the tools I use in my practice is called the SMART Life Chart. I use it as an exercise to help people recognize where they are putting their attention and energy. It is a way for people to distinguish if they are effectively balancing their time and energy with work, family life, and the other commitments they have.

Mary Ellen is a thirty-eight-year-old mother of two children. She has been married for twelve years. She is active in her community, often volunteering for the local book festival and a charity run to fight breast cancer. She went back to work when her youngest child started kindergarten three years ago. She was beginning to have trouble balancing it all.

At her first session, she described feeling overwhelmed by her commitments and that most mornings she felt "mommy guilt" even though she tried to only work when her children were in school. She has quickly moved up as an editor for a local magazine and hasn't been able to work from home as she would have liked. She didn't want to quit her job; she loves working and believes she is much happier with a job than being a stay-at-home mom. She admitted that she overcommits herself, and did so even when she was home with her children for five years. Clearly, quitting her job was not the answer.

When we reviewed the many ways Mary Ellen has tried to improve her ability to balance her life, she told me about all the gadgets she had purchased to keep herself organized. With the amount of time she spent learning how to program a PalmPilot and the charts she used for her calendar on the refrigerator, it is no wonder she was feeling so overwhelmed. She was giving herself the message of ineffectiveness, and it seemed as if she was only making matters worse. Mary Ellen's problem was not one of time management; it was one of balancing her attention and energy.

As we drew her SMART Life Chart, Mary Ellen identified the areas where she most needed to put her attention and energy. This was a difficult concept for her to grasp since she, like most people, tended to talk about time. When Mary Ellen was finally able to think outside the concept of time, the exercise was much easier for her. She identified the areas of children, marriage, and personal development. Collectively, we would categorize these things as "family life." She then identified her work life as "career/job and community activities,"since she considered her volunteer work fulfilling, but also an energy drain.

SMART Life Chart
Attention & Energy

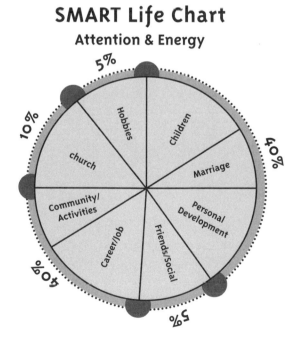

Before we continued to identify what would go into the Life Chart, I asked her to consider that she was trying to put equal amounts of attention and energy into her work life and family life, and, therefore, the percentage we indicated for both should be equal as well. We agreed on 40

percent for each since she believed that 80 percent of her total attention and energy should be divided between work and home commitments.

After many questions to help Mary Ellen identify where her energy and attention flows, Mary Ellen identified her intention to preserve attention and energy for her hobbies (she was a committed scrapbooker and exerciser), church (she worked in the nursery and participated in church activities), and friends (she had friends from college and wanted to stay in touch with them). It was important for Mary Ellen to decide how much attention and energy of the leftover 20 percent should be allocated to each of the remaining categories. Even though the numbers may not be exact, these percentages are estimates of where she should intentionally try to place her attention and energy in order to try and achieve the balance she so desperately wanted. By being selfish with what she agreed to do, it was possible for Mary Ellen to develop the kind of lifestyle that she wanted with less "mommy guilt" and less of a struggle balancing it all.

Here are some examples of other things that could be included as distinct categories in the SMART Life Chart:
- Caring for elderly parents
- Exercise
- Weight loss
- College classes
- Writing a book
- Trying to conceive a child
- "Emptying your bucket"

Emptying Your Bucket

What about managing stress? The old adages of "counting to ten" and "taking a breath" are insufficient tools for balancing work and family life. Most of the people I see in my practice who rely on those strategies tell me that they are ineffective when they are under stress. Let's take a look at stress management another way—a smarter way; one that relies on shifting the way you think, rather than changing your actions first. You change the way you think and your actions will follow.

I believe everybody has a bucket inside of them. When something causes stress, frustrates you, makes you angry, or just requires a lot of attention and energy, the bucket starts to fill. It is important to be aware of whether or not your bucket is full, because when it fills up completely, people have what I call an exaggerated response. An exaggerated response is when you overreact to whatever the trigger is at the time. You know you are having an exaggerated response when people look at you like you are weird or out of control. Then you start to realize you are wigging out or, as some kids call it, "losing it." Typically when your bucket is full, even small things can trigger an exaggerated response. You may be in a camera store picking up your photos when it happens. You expected they would be ready in an hour, and you're told it will be a few more minutes. Because your bucket is full, you are likely to overreact. If your bucket wasn't full, the extra time it will take might not be so aggravating. I believe most people don't know when their bucket is full and, more important, they don't know what to do to empty it. To put yourself and your family first, it would be important to know.

SMART Bucket

There are many things that can fill your bucket. You could be worried about a sick child, you could have a deadline looming at work, you could be in the middle of remodeling your home, or you could be trying to lose twenty pounds. Sometimes we can anticipate when our bucket will get full. For me, even preparing for a vacation can fill my bucket—especially getting things together for a road trip with three small boys. If you can anticipate something that will fill your bucket, you can get ahead of it. I no longer try and pack each night a little at a time. It used to be the way I emptied my bucket, but ultimately, when I realized that wasn't the most efficient way to get organized, I went to a new strategy. Now when we get ready to go on vacation, we plan it so I can have one day to get organized before we set out for the trip and one day to get organized right after we return from the trip. The laundry alone is enough to fill anyone's bucket. If I protect time for all my organizational needs, I keep ahead of my bucket and am able to limit my exaggerated responses.

Here are other things that tend to fill people's buckets:
- A long commute to work
- Standardized testing for their school-aged child
- A lack of resources
- Being asked to do more at work with fewer resources
- Being sick
- Financial stressors
- Environmental stressors
- Difficult relationships
- Difficult employees
- Difficult spouse
- Sibling rivalry
- Learning a new skill

When I am asked to talk about staying in the SMART Zone in community settings, for corporations, or conferences, I hear a lot of great ideas for emptying your bucket.

Some of those suggestions include the following:
- Getting enough sleep
- Exercise
- Spending quality time with family
- Spending quality time with friends
- Church involvement

- Community involvement
- Meditation
- Reading
- Staying organized

These ideas can even be taught to your children, so they too can learn how to balance it all and put the important things first. It is much better to say to your child, "Your bucket is full. Let's figure out a way to empty it," rather than, "What is wrong with you? Can't you handle it?"

There are some ways parents try to empty their bucket in search of temporary relief, but I believe some of these things might eventually be recycled, and go on to quickly fill that bucket to the brim.

Some of the poor choices for emptying your bucket can include:
- Affairs
- Alcohol abuse
- Substance abuse (illegal and prescription)
- Excessive withdrawal from social activities and groups
- Antisocial activities
- Smoking
- Stealing
- Gambling
- Gossip
- Overeating

The time with our families is precious. Make sure you are not chasing the years of your life.

Chasing the Years of Your Life

As I have mentioned already, someone once suggested to me that we are raising the parents of our grandchildren. If you break your life cycle into four stages, consider this: The first stage is our own childhood and adolescence, during which, for approximately eighteen years (for some of you, it might have been longer), we live under the physical guidance of our parents. During the second stage, we are typically on our own until we get married. The third stage is building our own family. And finally, the fourth stage is the empty-nest stage, when our children are out on their own. Of course, there are other stages in between, but for the purposes of putting family first, consider all perspectives.

We only live one hundred years, and of those years, we get only eighteen in close proximity to our children, when we have the ability to guide them day to day. In the big picture, our time with our families is precious. Stay in your SMART Zone; don't chase the years of your life.

SMART Moves:

- Make sure that your needs are met so that you can better meet the needs of your child.

- In order to put your family first, you must learn to balance your attention and energy in all aspects of your life—this is SMART life management.

- To avoid overreactions and exaggerated responses to stressful situations, try and empty your bucket before it overflows.

- Some ideas that help empty your bucket include: getting enough sleep, exercising, spending quality time with family and friends, meditation, and reading.

Glossary

Anxiety Disorder: Reaction to stress that becomes excessive and often interferes with daily functioning.

Attention-Deficit/Hyperactivity Disorder (AD/HD): A condition affecting children and adults that is characterized by problems with attention, impulsivity, and overactivity. It affects between 3-7 percent of school-age children, and between 2-4 percent of adults.

Attention Fix: In the case of repeated misbehavior, a child's need for attention from a parent. The child may continue the behavior seeking satisfaction until the behavior is no longer satisfying or necessary.

Bucket Inside You: A metaphor for the ever-present receptor of stress that fills frequently. The bucket's contents need to be emptied often to avoid the bucket getting full and possibly precipitating an exaggerated response.

Character: Inherent complex of attributes that determine a person's moral and ethical actions and reactions.

Collaborative Parenting: Parents working jointly for the benefit of the goal.

Content: The topic or "reasons" in a conversation or argument. This changes frequently and tends to be symbolic. Many times it is irrelevant; too frequently it is the focus for resolution.

Daily Parenting Hassles: Term coined by Keith Crnic, Ph.D. describing routine caregiving and childrearing responsibilities that parents may find irritating, frustrating, annoying, and distressing.

Depression: An illness that involves the body, mind, and thoughts, and often interferes with normal functioning.

Discipline: Investment in positive, long-lasting improvement in future behavior; implies that a parent's job is to teach.

Emotional Distance Model: Illustrates the emotional attachment or degree of engagement between two people. Illustrates the idea that relationships without the appropriate emotional distance tend to be unstable.

Emotional Intelligence: The capacity for recognizing our own feelings and those of others, motivating ourselves, and managing emotions in ourselves and in our relationships.

Exaggerated Response: When a person overreacts to a stressor that is not significant enough for such an explosive response.

Expectation Management: Deliberately attempting to be realistic in expected outcomes.

Extinguishing Behavior: Providing an environment where a child's negative behavior fades and no longer serves a purpose or is necessary for attention.

Facilitative Feedback: A communication skill where a person parrots back what has just been said.

Flow: The state of deep focus that occurs when people engage in challenging tasks that demand intense concentration and commitment.

Friendship: The ability to form and maintain close personal relationships with individual members of the peer group.

Group Acceptance: Being liked by your peers and feeling a part of a group.

High-Value Items: Everyday opportunities that matter and are not negotiable for a child's well-being or the functioning of a family. Typically the main focus for most families.

Hot Reactor: Having harsh reactions and being quick to respond in conversation.

Hugging the Tree: Staying focused on the main point and on-task in conversations, especially during arguments.

Internal Sense Of Pride: Developing and knowing yourself that you have done a good job without needing to be told by external sources.

Learning Disability: Specific neurological disorders that affect the brain's ability to store, process, or communicate information. Learning disabilities affect approximately 5 percent of all children enrolled in public schools.

Locus of Control: The extent to which an individual believes his or her behavior determines specific life events.

Low-Value Items: Everyday opportunities to expect compliance or negotiation where children can learn to be responsive and contribute positively to their own well-being or the functions of a family. Tend to be less valuable but more important in mass and over time. Unfortunately not the main focus for most families.

Low-Value SMART Model: Model that illustrates how to foster self-initiated responsible behaviors by reinforcing low-value items more often than high-value items.

Micromanage: Heavy supervision from external sources introduced at the expense of the development of internal resources and abilities.

Non-Negotiable Necessities: Behaviors or preferences that reflect your core values and are difficult to bend or adjust. These should be honored and respected; going against them causes turmoil.

Parental Mission Statement: Unified expression of your parenting philosophy; the principles you chose to govern your parenting decisions.

Personality: An individual's unique constellation of consistent behavior traits.

Process: The "take a step back and look at what is going on" part of a conversation or argument. It typically stays the same and tends to be the target for repairs in a relationship.

Parenting with a Hammer: "Losing your cool" with an emotional intensity that ultimately inhibits a child's ability to communicate effectively.

Privacy: The state of being free from unsanctioned intrusion. Implies something personal that is allowed and not forbidden.

Punishment: Tends to set limitations, involve power over a child, and interfere with creating an environment where a child can learn from mistakes.

Regulating Emotions: Staying in control of the intensity of your emotions and how they affect your behavior.

Repairing the Relationship: Making attempts to acknowledge differences and coexist in a satisfactory way in a relationship.

Resolving an Argument: Trying to get the other person to see your point of view at the expense of the relationship.

Secrecy: Implies the concept of concealment and something being hidden, implying the possibility of malicious intent.

Self-Efficacy: The expectation that people hold about their abilities to accomplish certain tasks.

Self-Esteem: The reputation we have with ourselves.

Self-Soothe: Calming yourself down and being in charge of your own emotions. No one can make you feel a certain way. You decide how you feel.

Sluggish Cognitive Tempo: Inconsistent alertness and orientation that is a subset of symptoms suggestive of Attention-Deficit/Hyperactivity Disorder (AD/HD).

SMART Internal Resources: A person's ability to self-soothe and problem-solve by his or her own means rather than relying solely on external resources for comfort.

SMART Life Cycle: A model for evaluating attention and energy in a deliberate and adaptable way.

SMART Life Management: More than life management, this is the ability to manage attention and energy to balance work and family life.

SMART Parenting: Parenting to the best of your ability in your SMART Zone.

SMART Parenting Philosophy: Your unique philosophy of parenting developed with the benefit of education, forethought, and consideration of long-term parenting goals.

SMART Sandwich Model: A structure for communicating that fosters more effective communication. Made up of several parts, including include acknowledging the expected responses, stating the "meat" of what you want to say, and an action statement connected by "ands" instead of "buts."

Social Competency: Peer relationships including group acceptance and friendships. Fosters a child's social understanding and individual development.

Temperament: An aspect of personality concerned with emotional dispositions and reactions and their speed and intensity. Often refers to the prevailing mood or mood pattern of a person.

Resources

Children And Adults With Attention-Deficit/Hyperactivity Disorder (CHADD)
8181 Professional Place, #150
Landover, Maryland 20785
(800) 233-4050
www.Chadd.org

Developing Capable People
(812) 334-0262
www.CapabilitiesInc.com

Learning Disabilities Association of America
4156 Library Road
Pittsburgh, Pennsylvania 15234-1439
(412) 341-1515
www.LDAAmerica.org

National Center for Learning Disabilities
381 Park Avenue South, #1401
New York, New York 10016
(888) 575-7373
www.ld.org

National Institute of Mental Health (NIMH)
6001 Executive Boulevard
Bethesda, Maryland 20892
(866) 615-6464
www.nimh.nih.gov

The Love and Logic Institute, Inc.
2207 Jackson St.
Suite 102
Golden, Colorado
80401-2300
www.LoveandLogic.com
1-800-LUV-LOGIC

About SMART Zone Productions

For information about products by Susan Fletcher, Ph.D. and her private practice visit www.FletcherPhD.com.

> **Book:** *Parenting in the SMART Zone*
> **Special Report Audio CD's** (See www.HearSusan.com for descriptions):
>   Attention-Deficit/Hyperactivity Disorder (AD/HD)
>   Childhood Depression
>   Learning Disabilities
>   Adult Depression

For information about hiring Susan Fletcher, Ph.D. as a speaker, please visit www.HearSusan.com.

> As a licensed psychologist currently in private practice and a sought-after professional speaker, Susan gets right to the point. Her presentations offer a new perspective to help others better manage change and increase productivity in their lives. Her dynamic presentations are uniquely tailored to the needs of each audience after careful collaboration with program planners and meeting professionals. Contact Susan for corporate programs, educational events, and other speaking opportunities. Susan will engineer the experience from beginning to end to develop the most valuable program possible.

For information: Susan Fletcher, Ph.D
  SMART Zone Productions
  2301 Ohio Drive, Suite 135
  Plano, Texas 75093
  (877) 447.8726

  Websites: www.HearSusan.com
       www.FletcherPhD.com

Ask about discounts for multiple products